Mars has been

flown by, orbited,

smacked into,

radar examined,

and rocketed onto,

as well as bounced upon,

rolled over, shoveled,

drilled into, baked, and even blasted.

Still to come:

Mars being stepped on.

—BUZZ ALDRIN

BUZZ ALDRIN

WELCOME TO

MARS

MAKING A HOME ON THE RED PLANET

With Marianne J. Dyson

NATIONAL
GEOGRAPHIC
KiDS

WASHINGTON, D.C.

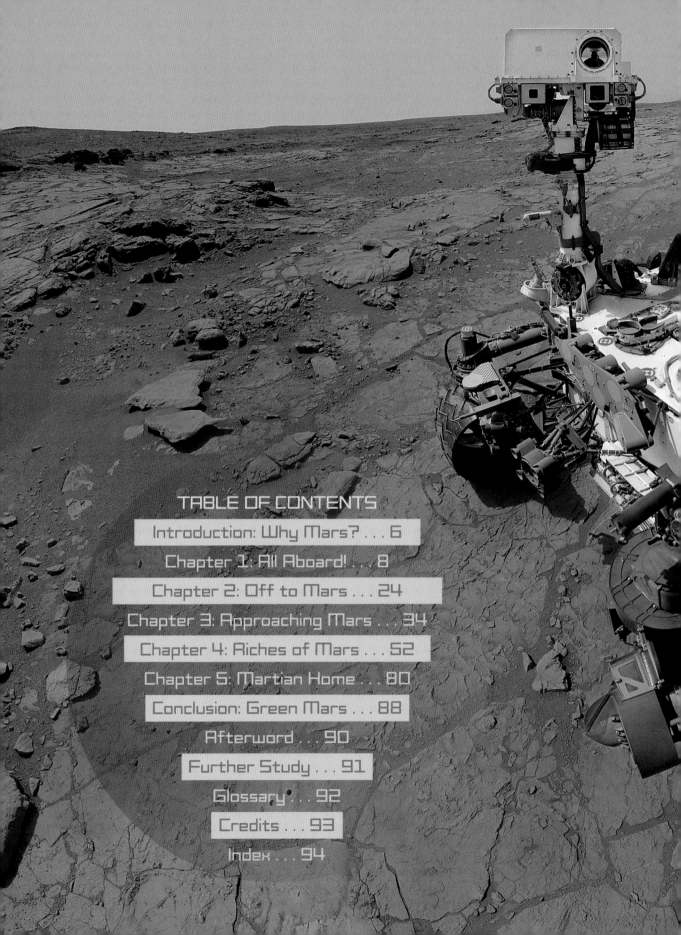

TABLE OF CONTENTS

WHY MARS?

People have built homes all over the Earth. More than half the world's people live in cities. I've visited log cabins in the mountains, stone castles in deep valleys, and adobe huts in the desert. I've joined sailors who make their homes on the sea. I even had the chance to live on the moon for a day. As long as people have air, water, food, and shelter, they can live anywhere. And soon, people just like you may decide to make their homes on Mars.

Mars is the only other world in our solar system that has everything we need. Venus is way too hot for us—about 850°F (450°C)! A giant sunshade might cool it off, but we'd still be crushed under its superthick air.

The moon is close and has metals and fuel. But nights are two weeks long, the gravity is minimal, and there is no air.

We could also live in space stations that spin around to make artificial gravity. But to build those, we need the soil, water, and minerals that asteroids and planets have to offer. Mars already has all of those things.

Mars is the most Earth-like planet in our solar system—besides Earth, of course. A day on Mars is about the same length as one on Earth. Mars has four seasons, though they are twice as long as Earth's. It has a solid surface with almost as much land area as Earth. Most important, Mars has water, even though the water is frozen.

But will people want to live on Mars? Some have already volunteered!

These pioneers will create new kinds of homes, maybe in domes or by putting roofs over canyons and craters. The low gravity and cold climate will let them invent new sports like snowboarding on dry ice. They'll adapt Earth plants to Martian soil and open restaurants serving alien food. The anniversary of their arrival will be a holiday for generations to celebrate.

The pioneers who settle Mars will also ensure the long-term survival of life in our solar system. Earth faces challenges. If there were a disaster, Mars would give us a place to get resources or to make a new home. The new and better ways the settlers will learn to grow food, clean the air, process metals, and recycle waste may even ease conflicts over resources on Earth.

Plans for building the first homes on Mars are already in progress. Through this book, you'll learn why I think it's time to commit ourselves to building a permanent home on the red planet.

THIS ART SHOWS THE MARS SCIENCE
LABORATORY ENTERING MARS'S ATMOSPHERE.

Chapter 1

ALL ABOARD!

ongratulations on becoming a Martian pioneer! And welcome to my crew. It will be our job to build the first city on Mars. This is an opportunity that will happen only once. You're lucky to be the right age to have this chance to make history!

A World
Far, Far Away

Going to Mars is sort of like choosing to attend college in another country or joining the military. Prepare to be gone from Earth for a long time. You won't get to go home for the holidays. You'll have to keep in touch by computer. You may even stay there permanently. But even if you wanted to go back to Earth from Mars, the shortest round-trip takes from a year and a half to two years and eight months, depending on where Mars is in its orbit around the sun. Why so long?

Mars is really far away. Really, really far. The distance is equal to about 10,000 trips around the Earth. When I went to the moon in 1969, it took us about three days to get there and three days to get back. Even at rocket speeds, it takes about six months to reach Mars. Then we would have to wait on (or orbit around) Mars 30 to 540 days for Mars's and Earth's orbits to line up if we need to send someone back.

But our job is to build the first permanent city on Mars. I'm counting on you to settle there. Let's build a home on Mars where families from around the world can live peacefully.

How many people will it take for us to build the first city? There were three of us on each Apollo flight to the moon. Two astronauts went to the surface while one stayed in orbit. But the space systems for Mars are much more complicated. They have to keep working for years—and that requires a lot of updating, cleaning, and fixing. We need at least two people to do that as well as to look after each other. We have to bring a buddy wherever we go in case we need help. So we should have a crew of at least four on any trip to Mars.

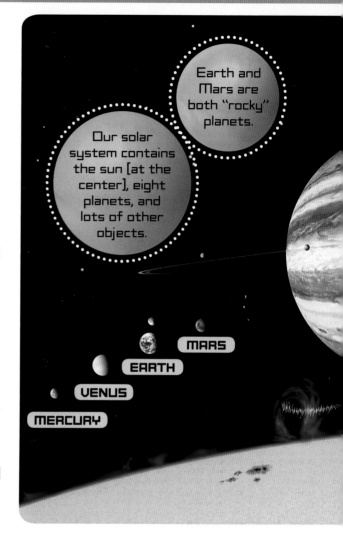

Earth and Mars are both "rocky" planets.

Our solar system contains the sun [at the center], eight planets, and lots of other objects.

MARS

EARTH

VENUS

MERCURY

But we want to get our new home built quickly. We also want two people trained for every job, and that's easier with more people. NASA's current plans for the first Mars flights suggest a crew of six. Larger crews will be possible after greenhouses and factories are working on Mars to support their needs. Setting those up will be our job!

So congratulations again on your selection to be a Martian pioneer. Our group has come from countries around the world. We'll have fun sharing our stories and learning about each other's customs as we travel to the red planet to build a new world together.

"Pack your **bags.** We've got a long, EXCITING JOURNEY ahead of us on the **RED PLANET.**"
—BRENDAN MULLAN, ASTROBIOLOGIST

JUPITER SATURN URANUS NEPTUNE

HERE I AM (ON THE RIGHT) WITH THE APOLLO 11 MOON-LANDING CREW. NEIL ARMSTRONG IS ON THE LEFT, AND MIKE COLLINS IS IN THE MIDDLE.

THE APOLLO 11 CREW PREPARES TO BOARD THEIR SPACECRAFT.

Your Favorite Five Pounds

What do you need to pack for our trip? We need a lot more than clothes, toothpaste, and snacks for our trip to Mars. There will be some things already there waiting for us, though. The first few crews will have set up temporary houses or habitats ("habs" for short) for us to live in. We'll have air and water from local Martian sources. The electrical power station will have come from Earth. Most of our food will come from greenhouses and underground mushroom farms. And I hope you like potatoes! We'll be eating lots of those.

Living off the land on Mars also means that most of what we have there will be made from what we can get on the planet itself. We'll eat the food and make fabrics from plants that can grow there and make products out of materials we can mine. That means you may not get to wear your favorite sports jersey, but it also means that we mostly just need to pack what's required to get us there. NASA estimates that each person needs about 10 pounds (4.5 kg) of air, water, and food every day. Let's see, 10 pounds times 30 days in a month times six months is ... 1,800 pounds (816 kg)! That's not going to fit in two suitcases and a carry-on!

But don't worry. The ship that will take us to Mars recycles air and water, so we'll take only a small amount. A few veggie rack gardens will also help reduce our grocery list. But we still have to take a lot of food. We also need space suits and tools and computers, things we can't easily make on Mars. So, like we did on Apollo, you can take only 5 pounds (2.3 kg) of personal items. In choosing your items, note that they all have to fit in your backpack!

THINGS YOU WON'T NEED ON MARS

Lawn mower

Why? There's nothing to mow on Mars! Any plants that humans grow on Mars will need to be in a greenhouse.

Coat Sure, Mars is cold. Really cold. But we'll have specially designed space suits that let humans live in those conditions.

Umbrella

Although Mars has major dust storms that rage around the planet, it never has rainstorms.

Bug spray No known life on Mars means no known bugs. So you can leave the bug spray on Earth.

Boat Though rovers and probes have found evidence of streambeds, there's no liquid water on Mars today.

THE DELTA IV HEAVY ROCKET LAUNCHES
WITH THE ORION CREW VEHICLE ATTACHED.

All Aboard!

Our trip begins with a launch from Earth to Earth orbit. When I went to the moon, everything we needed for our trip was loaded on top of one big rocket. But our trip was just over eight days long. If we'd had to take enough groceries for six people for six months, the rocket could not have lifted off the launchpad!

And today's rockets aren't as powerful as the Saturn V that took me to the moon. The Saturn V boosted the weight of ten school buses into Earth orbit. The two biggest rockets available now are the American Delta IV Heavy and the Russian Proton-M. These rockets can each lift the weight of two buses into orbit around Earth.

NASA and some private companies are working on more powerful rockets. If successful, the rockets may be available by 2021. But even so, it will not be possible to launch everything needed for a Mars landing in one go. Instead, NASA is planning to launch its biggest rocket four times, each time with different cargo. All of this cargo will then be sent on ahead toward Mars. Once all that is assembled in orbit (remotely from Earth), we head for our "taxi" ride to space.

When you see the bill for this taxi ride, you might be shocked. It costs tens of millions of dollars to get to orbit. How could you afford that? Maybe you can model sports socks or sell mining rights to your property on Mars? Sell your story to a reality TV show? Sell everything you're not taking with you? However you pay for it, one question everyone asks is, "Why is it so expensive to launch people into space?!"

First Class Only

There are two main reasons why launching people into space is expensive. One, it's hard! Rockets have to reach speeds of five miles (8 km) per second. They also have to protect people against the temperatures and lack of air in space. To do that, they have to provide backup systems. On Earth, if your car runs out of fuel, you can walk to a gas station for more. If the air-conditioning fails, you can open windows. In a rocket, if you run out of fuel, you crash. If the AC fails, you can't breathe. So in space you need two or more of all the equipment that keeps you alive in case of failures. It takes a lot of time (and money) to build and test these systems and train astronauts to use them. Cargo rockets don't need all this extra equipment. If the rocket crashes, the cargo can be replaced. Replacing cargo is expensive, but people are priceless!

The second reason launching people is expensive is the lack of competition. When you go to buy a car, you have lots of choices. The car dealers compete to get your business. When it comes to rockets, you have several choices for cargo. But there is currently only one choice for crew. The United States retired its space shuttles in 2011. Since then, the U.S. has had to pay the Russian government more than $70 million per person to

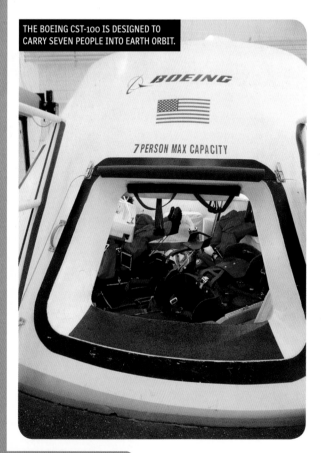

THE BOEING CST-100 IS DESIGNED TO CARRY SEVEN PEOPLE INTO EARTH ORBIT.

THE SPACEX DRAGON CAPSULE DELIVERS CARGO TO THE INTERNATIONAL SPACE STATION.

THE RUSSIAN SOYUZ IS USED TO TAKE CREWS TO AND FROM THE INTERNATIONAL SPACE STATION.

"In the next few decades, I plan to travel to **Mars** and make it my home." —Elon Musk, founder, SpaceX

take astronauts to the International Space Station (ISS) and back. The only other rocket that can take people up is the Chinese Long March. No Americans have ever flown on a Chinese rocket. To use that option, we'd need some new international agreements.

NASA is working on a crew capsule called Orion. This capsule may fly four astronauts to space in 2021. American companies are also working on vehicles that would take up to seven people to orbit. Some of these may be ready even sooner.

View from Phobos

The first crews to go to Mars might not land on the surface. They may go to one of the two Martian moons.

Astronomers named these moons Phobos (fear) and Deimos (panic)—good companions for Mars, the god of war. But there's no need for fear or panic! These small moons offer a natural place from which to study Mars.

A mission to Phobos could be for Mars like the Apollo 8 mission was for the moon. For Apollo 8, in 1968, humans orbited, but didn't land on, the moon. It was a test run. The crew of Apollo 8 were the first to ride a Saturn V booster into space. They were the first to fly a spacecraft into orbit around the moon—and see it up close with their own eyes. They sent back spectacular photos and gathered data to help scientists pick the best place for me and Neil Armstrong to land the following year.

We could do something similar with Phobos. A mission to Phobos could be a "shakedown" cruise for a Mars transport vehicle, taking its crew to higher speeds and farther from Earth than ever before. We could learn a lot from that. A Phobos mission could also be less expensive than landing on Mars. A crew of four could do it, reducing the amount of needed supplies.

Phobos is too small to have an atmosphere or much gravity—just enough to define "up" and "down." If you jump too high off the surface, you would have to wait a very long time to be pulled back down! The surface is also covered with fine dust that would spray everywhere if you tried to walk through it. So astronauts visiting Phobos may fly around just above the surface using jet packs that are mounted in a frame. All that dust is a good thing, though—astronauts might use it for radiation protection.

Scientists don't know if there is water under the surface on Phobos. If there is, Phobos may become one of the solar system's first "gas" stations! There's one thing we know we'll find on Phobos, though: sunlight. There is a place near the rim that has nearly constant sunlight. This sunlight will provide electrical power for our crew.

From Phobos, an astronaut can see areas near the equator of Mars for about four hours in a row (half of an eight-hour orbit). The polar areas of Mars are not visible from Phobos because it is only 3,700 miles (5,955 km) from Mars. (Earth's moon is 240,000 miles [386,242 km] away from Earth.) And Phobos is getting closer to Mars all the time. In fact, Phobos will

THE FACTS

Phobos	
SIZE	8 miles (13 km) by 7 miles (11 km) by 5.5 miles (9 km)
ORBITAL PERIOD	7 hours 39 minutes
ALTITUDE ABOVE MARS	3,721 miles (5,950 km)

Deimos	
SIZE	4.7 miles (7.5 km) by 4 miles (6 km) by 3 miles(5 km)
ORBITAL PERIOD	30 hours 18 minutes
ALTITUDE ABOVE MARS	12,468 miles (20,066 km)

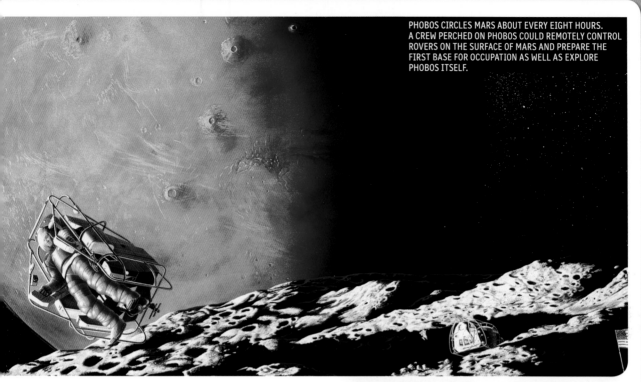

PHOBOS CIRCLES MARS ABOUT EVERY EIGHT HOURS. A CREW PERCHED ON PHOBOS COULD REMOTELY CONTROL ROVERS ON THE SURFACE OF MARS AND PREPARE THE FIRST BASE FOR OCCUPATION AS WELL AS EXPLORE PHOBOS ITSELF.

eventually crash into Mars. But don't worry! Nearing at a rate of six feet (1.8 m) every 100 years, Phobos will take 50 million years to hit Mars. Humans, on the other hand, can zip down in our spacecraft in a matter of hours. Also, if we want to check out the poles from orbit, we can go to Deimos, or use orbiting satellites.

From Phobos's surface in orbit around Mars, astronauts can control rovers on Mars. These rovers might pick up samples the crew can study. Are there Martian microbes or chemicals in the dust that could make people sick? Is there enough water near the surface for people to drink and to grow crops? How hard is it to make fuel from Martian air? Where is the best place to land?

The crew might also set up the first human base by remote control, depending on what equipment is sent ahead or with them. They could guide a habitat and power plant to a landing place they select. A greenhouse and supplies from Earth could be added and

PHOBOS

tested. Astronauts on Phobos could do in a few weeks what it took rovers controlled from Earth five years to do.

Once the surface base is ready to support people, the Phobos crew may fly down and become the first permanent settlers. The transport that brought them might be left in orbit to use in case of an emergency. But if all goes well on the surface, the transport might be reused to bring the next crew: us!

ACTIVITY: RACE AROUND THE CLOCK

The Earth and Mars are like the hands of a clock, going around the sun at the center. But unlike a clock, the "short" hand goes around faster. Earth is on a track closer to the sun than Mars is. It orbits the sun faster than Mars does. Try this activity to see how often Earth and Mars pass each other as they race around the sun.

SUPPLIES

- A piece of cardboard that is 8 inches [20 cm] square
- A marker or pen
- A tape measure or yardstick [meterstick]
- Two small toy cars, preferably blue for Earth and red for Mars!
- Two pieces of string or yarn, one about 20 inches [50 cm] long, and one about 25 inches [63.5 cm] long
- A round pencil, preferably not sharpened
- Tape

CREATE THE CLOCK

1 Fold the cardboard lengthwise and then open it up. Draw a line in the fold.

2 Fold the cardboard widthwise, open it up, and draw a line in the fold. This line should cross the other line. Mark the center with a big dot or an X. This is the position of the sun.

3 Now use the tape measure or yardstick to mark out the times on the clock. First, measure 3 inches (7.6 cm) from the sun in all four directions marked by the lines. Place dots there. These are the 12, 3, 6, and 9 positions of the clock.

4 Now add the rest of the numbers to the clock. Measure 3 inches (7.6 cm) out from the center and place two numbers between each of the numbers already on the clock. For example, place dots 3 inches out from the center to mark 1 and 2 between the 12 and 3 positions.

5 Connect all the dots to make a circle.

6 Poke a hole in the center of the clock and push the pencil through so the eraser end is on the backside of the clock. Tape it in place.

7 Tie one end of the 25-inch (63.5-cm) piece of string around the pencil. Knot it so it won't come loose when tugged on. Add the 20-inch (50-cm) string to the pencil above the longer string. Stretch the strings out to one side.

8 Lay the tape measure or yardstick with 0 at the pencil "sun." Tie or tape the shorter string to the Earth car at a distance of 10 inches (25 cm) from the sun.

9 Tie or tape the longer string to the Mars car at a distance of 15 inches (38 cm) from the sun.

1

2

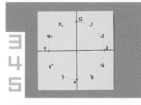
3 4 5

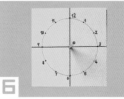
6

7

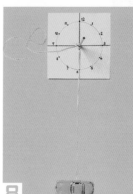
8

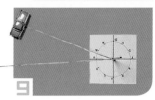
9

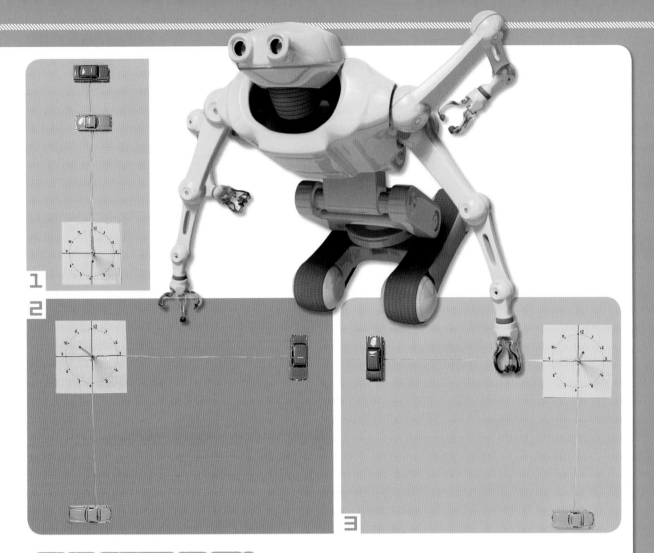

THE RACE IS ON

1 Place Mars and Earth on the "starting line" at 12. Earth moves one clock "hour" each month. Mars moves about half that much.

Note: The planets move around the sun "backward" or counterclockwise, as seen from "above" looking "down" on the solar system from the north. (Earth moves from 12 to 11 to 10.) But to keep from having to count backward, we're going to move Earth and Mars clockwise (from 12 to 1 to 2), which is how it looks from "below," looking "up" at the solar system.

2 Move the cars through 6 months. Earth should be at 6 on the clock, and Mars at 3. Move another 6 months (a year has passed). Earth is back at 12, and Mars is at 6. Note that this is as far apart as they can be and that the sun is between Earth and Mars. Would this be a good time to look at Mars through a telescope from Earth?

3 Move another 6 months (18 months have passed). Earth is back at 6. Mars is at 9. If we were sending a ship to Mars, why would this be a good time to launch it? (Hint: It takes a ship about 6 months to cross the gap between Earth and Mars, and it can't go straight across.)

4 Move another 6 months (2 years have passed). Earth and Mars are both at 12 again. How long will it be before Earth and Mars are in this position again? Would this be a good time to look at Mars through a telescope?

The Aldrin Cycler

The best time to go to Mars occurs every two years and two months. If we try to go to Mars at other times, it either takes a lot longer to get there, or it takes more energy than our rockets have to offer. This launch "window" makes it hard to build a permanent place on Mars very quickly. Launching a transport from Earth orbit and slowing it down at Mars, and then doing the reverse, requires a lot of fuel. The amount of fuel needed dwarfs everything else we have to take, including your six months' worth of lunches. If we want to settle Mars, we need to get this cost down. One way to do it is to set up an interplanetary "railroad" like we did when we settled the American West.

The "track" is already laid for us by nature. I discovered this when I was studying space rendezvous, the meeting of two things in space. Earth and Mars always follow the same paths around the sun. And there are paths between Earth and Mars that repeat in a cycle. If we put a spacecraft

1 Month 1: As the outbound cycler passes through Earth orbit, the crew lifts off from Earth in an ascent vehicle to meet it.

2 About 6 months: The cycler crosses Mars orbit. The crew takes a descent vehicle to Mars's surface.

3 About 20 months: As the outbound cycler continues on its path, it crosses Mars orbit again. Mars is not here, though. In order to have a cycler meet Mars at this point in its orbit, a second [inbound] cycler would be launched from Earth.

4 About 26 months: Two years and two months after first passing Earth, the outbound cycler is again in Earth's orbit, and a new crew can lift off from Earth to meet it.

RENDEZVOUS WITH GEMINI

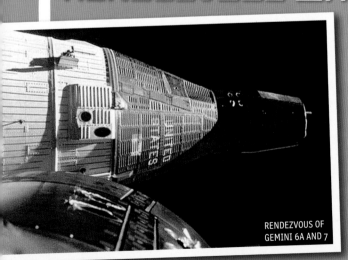

RENDEZVOUS OF GEMINI 6A AND 7

I was an Air Force pilot stationed in Germany when the Soviet Union—a country that included what is now Russia—launched the first spacecraft, called Sputnik, in 1957. I realized that space was going to play an important part in the future. So after my tour of duty in Germany, I went back to college to learn more about space.

The Soviets launched the first human into space on April 12, 1961. The first American space flight was on May 5 of that year. But this flight just went up and came back down. It didn't go all the way around the Earth. The

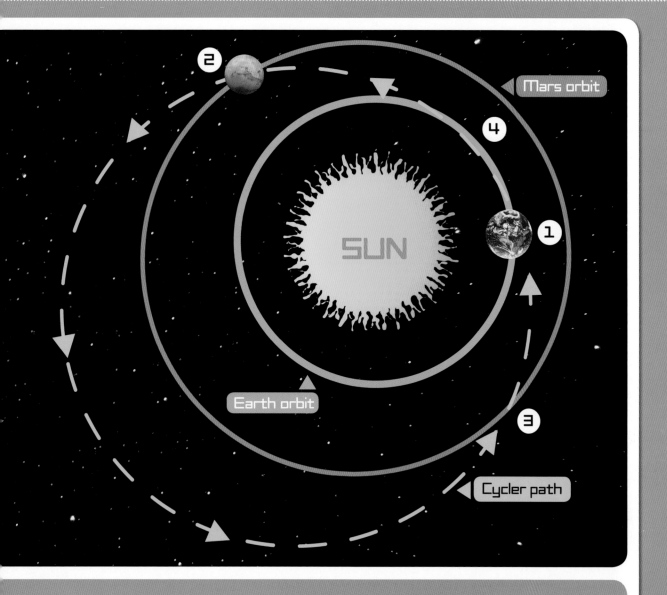

2

Mars orbit

4

1

SUN

Earth orbit

3

Cycler path

Soviets had better rockets! The U.S. was determined to catch up. On May 25, 1961, President F. John Kennedy set the goal of landing men on the moon before 1970.

Kennedy's speech inspired me. I joined NASA in 1963. NASA had a program called Gemini to test rendezvous—that was my expertise. The first rendezvous was between Gemini 6A and 7 in 1965.

I flew with Jim Lovell on Gemini 12 in November 1966. During our flight, the guidance radar went down. I had to do all the math in my head! But it gave me a chance to test out the theories about rendezvous I had developed, and they worked! These ideas would be important later when I developed cyclers for Mars.

SELFIE FROM GEMINI!

on such a path, it will cycle between Earth and Mars naturally, just as the planets circle the sun without the need for rocket fuel. The key is to use the pull of each world's gravity, like grabbing a pole to swing around and change direction. Once we get a set of these "trains" running, we can catch a ride to Mars every two years like clockwork. And every time we use it, we save having to launch at least four supersized rockets' worth of fuel.

I call these "trains" cyclers because they cycle back and forth between Earth and Mars. Because one cycler (inbound) will be on the way back to Earth while another (outbound) is going to Mars, we'll need at least two. (In honor of my Apollo friends, I want to name the first two Armstrong and Conrad.)

Because the cycler has to support six people for the six-month trip to Mars, it will be big. The International Space Station, which has been orbiting Earth for 15 years, provides life support for six people for six months without resupply.

So basically, the first Mars cycler might look like the early International Space Station. We could build something like this in less than three years. All of these modules and systems have been supporting people in space successfully for more than ten years.

As on the space station, solar arrays would power the cycler. New large, inflatable habitation modules are planned to be tested on the station soon. We could use those to house larger crews on the cycler.

The outbound cycler will have at least one part that the space station doesn't have: a Mars lander. This lander will transport our crew to Mars, like a taxi that takes us from the train station to our house. This lander may be similar to the lunar module that Neil and I rode to the surface of the moon. Whatever design we use, we'll be landing near the temporary base to learn more about Mars from the first crew. Then we'll pick up our supplies and head out to build a permanent home on the red planet.

ACTIVITY: LET GRAVITY DO THE WORK!

A planet's gravity pulls stronger the closer you get to it. As spacecraft get closer to Mars, gravity pulls harder and speeds them up. If a spacecraft is not aimed directly at Mars, it speeds up and sails past. After it passes, gravity still pulls on the spacecraft, like a ball thrown up in the air falls back toward Earth. Depending on how fast it is going when it swings back around, the spacecraft can land, go into orbit, or fly past in a new direction. The Aldrin cyclers will be aimed exactly so they go past and then swing around Mars and head back toward Earth. Do this activity to see how the speed changes where the cycler goes.

SUPPLIES

- Lots of open space
- Coin
- Large nonbreakable bowl, such as a mixing bowl

The Aldrin Cycler Spacecraft

[Outbound, Earth to Mars]

Habitation modules

Solar arrays

Solar electric propulsion

DIRECTIONS

1. Go to a place where a flying coin is not going to hit a person, pet, or anything breakable.

2. Put the coin with a flat side against the bowl near the top. Let it drop. See how gravity pulls a slow "spacecraft" down to the surface.

3. Hold the bowl in both hands by the edges. Swirl it around and around. Gradually increase your speed. As the coin goes faster, note its "orbit" rises up the side of the bowl. When it reaches "escape velocity," watch out! The coin will fly out of the bowl, on its way back to Earth!

Chapter 2

OFF TO MARS

As we head toward Mars, I think about the red planet. Did you know that Mars got its name because of its color? Ancient people thought it was red like blood, so they named it Mars after their god of war.

Mars is actually a peaceful place. It's red because the iron in its rocks is all rusted, like an old iron gate.

But we didn't know that when I was young. Back then, we thought that there might be intelligent beings on Mars, and that they might even wage war on us!

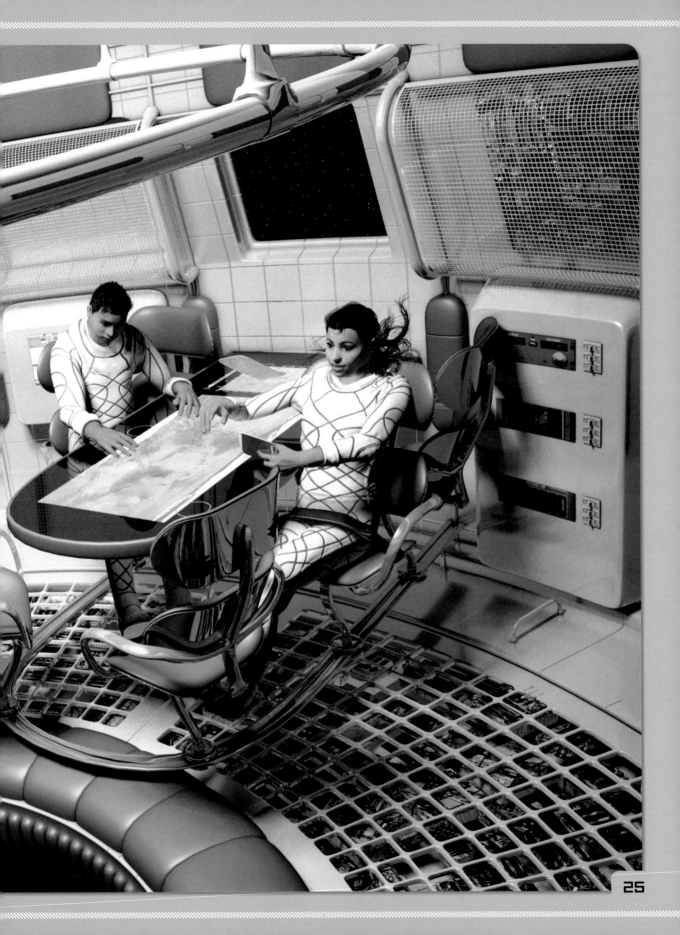

Martians
Invade Earth!

I was eight years old when the "Martians" attacked New Jersey. It was Halloween of 1938. That day, I was kicking a football around with some friends after school. The other kids said that monsters from Mars had landed in New Jersey, not far from our town. They'd heard it on the radio!

They weren't the only ones. Millions of listeners heard that "a huge, flaming object, believed to be a meteorite, fell on a farm in the neighborhood of Grovers Mill, New Jersey." A little while later, the radio announcer said it was a metal cylinder. It "rotates like a screw." Then, the breathless reporter said, "Wait a minute! Someone's crawling. Someone or … something. I can see peering out of that black hole two luminous disks … are they eyes? It might be a face. It might be … good heavens, something's wriggling out of the shadow like a gray snake. Now it's another one, and another one … They look like tentacles to me … It's large as a bear and it glistens like wet leather. But that face, it … ladies and gentlemen, it's indescribable. I can hardly force myself to keep looking at it, it's so awful."

What a lot of people didn't know was that the "reporter" was an actor. Martians were not attacking: It was a story based on the book *The War of the Worlds*, by H. G. Wells. The radio show had announced this at the beginning. But many people missed the announcement. They tuned in to hear that Martians were killing people with a "heat ray." They heard fake politicians say New York City was being evacuated. They panicked!

I soon learned that the "attack" wasn't real. But I still wondered if there might be real Martians up there in space.

In *The War of the Worlds*, Martians attack Earth.

Another name for Mars, the god of war, is Ares. The study of Mars is called areology.

THE WAR OF THE WORLDS, BY H.G. WELLS, WAS PUBLISHED IN 1898.

THE WAR OF THE WORLDS

H. G. WELLS

LOOKING GLASS LIBRARY

THIS ART OF *THE WAR OF THE WORLDS* SHOWS MARTIAN WALKERS SHOOTING "HEAT RAYS."

FAKE RADIO 'WAR' STIRS TERROR THROUGH U.S.

ACTOR ORSON WELLES DRAMATIZED *THE WAR OF THE WORLDS* ON A RADIO BROADCAST IN 1938. SOME PEOPLE THOUGHT IT WAS AN ACTUAL NEWS REPORT.

Canals on Mars

Back in 1938, we didn't have very good maps of Mars. Spacecraft hadn't been invented yet. The only way to view Mars was with a telescope.

The first maps were made by Italian astronomer Giovanni Schiaparelli in 1877. He looked through his telescope and sketched what he saw: dark lines on the surface of Mars. He labeled these *canali*, which means "channels" in Italian. The Suez Canal in Egypt had been completed only eight years earlier in 1869. A canal is a channel of water made by people. So people thought the canali on Mars must be canals, too. But if there were canals on Mars, who built them?

Wealthy American businessman Percival Lowell knew the answer: Martians! He shared his excitement about Mars with everyone. And people listened.

Everyone knew who Percival Lowell was. He wasn't just rich; he was Harvard educated and had traveled the world. He wrote for popular magazines. His books about Mars were translated and sold around the world. People flocked to hear him speak. If television had been invented then, he'd have been on all the talk shows.

Despite Lowell's fame, some scientists disagreed with him. They didn't think the lines were canals. They thought they were cracks in the surface that formed as Mars dried out. They suggested that these natural features only looked like lines from far away.

Lowell did his best to prove that the canals and Martians were real. He built an observatory in Arizona. He drew lots of maps showing the canals. He claimed that he saw Mars better than others because the skies

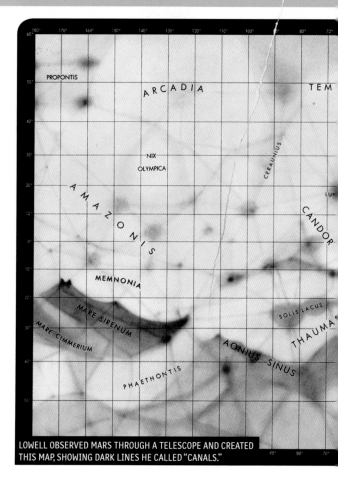

LOWELL OBSERVED MARS THROUGH A TELESCOPE AND CREATED THIS MAP, SHOWING DARK LINES HE CALLED "CANALS."

are so clear in Arizona. Lowell also hired a man to figure out how to take photos through the telescope. This had never been done before, but Lowell successfully did it in 1905. Even skeptics saw some lines in these tiny quarter-inch photos.

But they still didn't think the lines were canals. They also thought Mars was too cold, and the air too thin, to support life.

Lowell argued that all life needed was water. He noted that some plants need only a brief thaw in summer to survive. Plants also grow in the thin air on top of mountains. Lowell observed that Mars's ice caps shrink in summer. He assumed the Martians built the canals to channel melted ice to

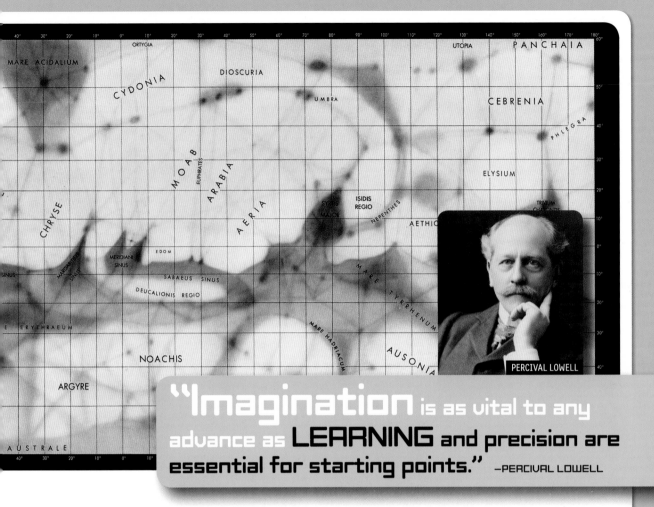

MARE ACIDALIUM
CYDONIA
ORTYGIA
DIOSCURIA
UMBRA
UTOPIA
PANCHAIA
CEBRENIA
PHLEGRA
MOAB
EUPHRATES
ARABIA
AERIA
ELYSIUM
ISIDIS REGIO
SYRTIS MAJOR
NEPENTHES
AETHIO
TRIVIUM CHARONTIS
CHRYSE
EDOM
MERIDIANI SINUS
MARGARITIFER SINUS
SINUS
SABAEUS SINUS
DEUCALIONIS REGIO
MARE TYRRHENUM
E ERYTHRAEUM
MARE HADRIACUM
AUSONIA
NOACHIS
ARGYRE
AUSTRALE

PERCIVAL LOWELL

"**Imagination** is as vital to any advance as **LEARNING** and precision are essential for starting points." —PERCIVAL LOWELL

water their crops. The crops growing along the canals made them appear dark.

Lowell invented a way to show that the air on Mars contains water. He attached a prism to his telescope. When light passes through a prism, it spreads out into a rainbow of colors called a spectrum. Water has its own special spectrum, or pattern of lines that appear through a prism. Lowell hired a man to find water in the spectrum of Mars.

This was not an easy task. All light coming from space has to pass through Earth's air, which is full of water. Looking for water from Mars was like watching for someone coming through a door at the end of the hall when the hall is full of people. So Lowell invented a

way to subtract the appearance of water in Earth's air. It was like clearing the hall of people. Finally, in 1908, Lowell had what he wanted: proof that Mars has water in its air.

Lowell used his maps and photos to show there were lines on Mars. He used spectra to show that Mars had water necessary for life. But he still couldn't prove the lines were canals or that Martians built them.

Bigger telescopes failed to find canals on Mars. Instead, with clearer images, they found dark features that weren't actually connected. But just because the lines weren't canals, astronomers couldn't say for sure there were no Martians. The only way to know was to visit Mars.

ACTIVITY: WHERE IS THE RED PLANET?

Mars is called the Red Planet because of its rusty color. You can see this color for yourself, and you don't even need a telescope!

You don't have to search the whole night sky to find Mars. Mars is always "in" one of 12 constellations that form a band around the Earth in the sky. A line running through the center of this ring is called the ecliptic (shown as a dashed line on star charts). The sun is always on this line, moving through one constellation's width each month. These constellations are called the signs of the zodiac. These are traditionally: Capricorn, Aquarius, Pisces, Aries, Taurus, Gemini, Cancer, Leo, Virgo, Libra, Scorpio,* and Sagittarius. (*The ecliptic has shifted since ancient times. After Scorpio, it now passes through Ophiuchus and then Sagittarius.)

Unfortunately, many of the stars of these constellations are dim and hard to find, especially if you live in a city. But you can still find the line that runs through them, and the track Mars follows, using the activity below.

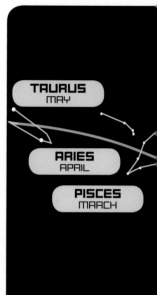

TAURUS
MAY

ARIES
APRIL

PISCES
MARCH

SUPPLIES

- A flashlight
- A compass
- A telescope or binoculars
- Your fist

USING THE ECLIPTIC TO FIND MARS

1 BE SAFE! Take a flashlight and ask an adult to go with you. The best time for observing Mars is when it is dark.

2 FIND NORTH. Use a compass, a cell phone app, the North Star, or the direction of sunrise (east) or sunset (west) to find north. Turn your back to the north and face south.

3 FIND THE ECLIPTIC. The ecliptic arches across the sky from east to west (left to right if you're facing south). If Mars isn't hiding behind the sun, it will appear somewhere on this imaginary line. The height of the line above the southern horizon depends on your latitude and the season. Use the graphic on page 31 to find the ecliptic in your region.

NOTE that though Mars is always on the ecliptic, it won't always be visible. Half of the ecliptic is on the "day" side of Earth. As the Earth rotates, a new "sign" rises in the east every two hours. So if you don't see Mars at night, check the eastern sky just before sunrise.

4 IDENTIFY MARS. Look along the ecliptic for a bright orange or reddish "star." If the light twinkles, it is not Mars. You can tell the difference between Mars and Jupiter by looking for moons with a telescope or binoculars. Jupiter has large moons that appear as bright dots in a line across its middle, whereas Mars's moons are too small to see. Saturn's rings are a dead giveaway! Venus is superbright and not orange. It also is never more than five fists above the east or west horizon.

THE ECLIPTIC

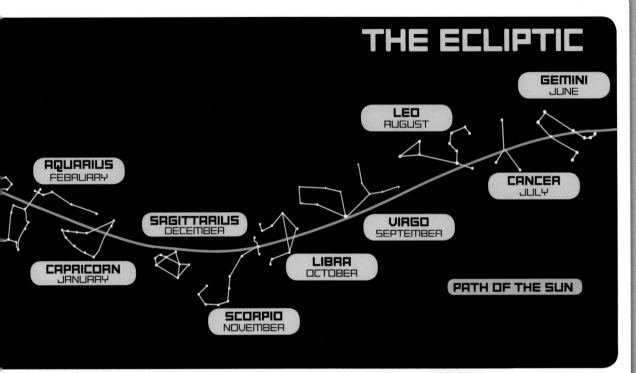

GEMINI
JUNE

LEO
AUGUST

AQUARIUS
FEBRUARY

CANCER
JULY

SAGITTARIUS
DECEMBER

VIRGO
SEPTEMBER

CAPRICORN
JANUARY

LIBRA
OCTOBER

PATH OF THE SUN

SCORPIO
NOVEMBER

SPRING AND FALL

A fist at arm's length is about 10 degrees. In the United States, the ecliptic is between five (northern states) and seven (southern states) fists above the southern horizon.

SUMMER AND WINTER

In summer and winter, the ecliptic tilts up to 23 degrees higher (summer) or lower (winter) during the day, and the same amount lower (summer) or higher (winter) at night. So in summer, the ecliptic will be three to five fists high in the United States at night. In the winter, it will be five to nine fists high. Nine fists high will be directly overhead.

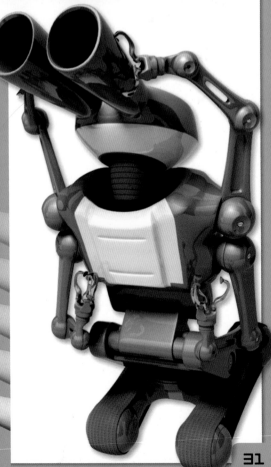

MARINER 4

Mars Flyby

When you observe Mars through our telescope here on the cycler, you won't see canals, but you might see a big gash across the middle. That's the Valles Marineris, named for the first spacecraft to visit Mars.

Mariner 4 reached Mars in the summer of 1964. I'd joined NASA the year before and had started training for my flight on Gemini 12. We were all anxious to see the photos of Mars up close sent by Mariner 4. Would Mars be similar to Earth's cratered moon? On July 14, Mariner 4 flew past Mars at a distance of about 6,000 miles (9,656 km). The first close-up photos finally proved that there were no canals. The photos didn't show any sign of green plants or Martians, either. Further exploration would have to wait, though. We were going to the moon!

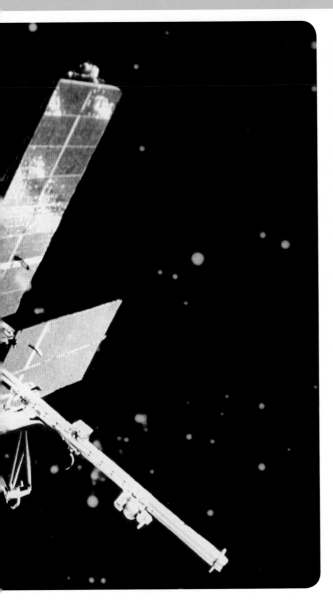

With all that failure, it seemed unsure. By 1968, though, we'd fixed the problems that had caused the accident. We tested the vehicles during four Apollo flights, two of which went around the moon, but didn't land.

Then, on July 20, 1969, Neil Armstrong and I landed on the moon. Being the first explorers to reach the moon was simply incredible. The surface was "magnificent desolation," I said. But exploring was also great fun. I almost wished that Neil and I had brought a baseball to toss back and forth a few times to demonstrate the effects of lunar gravity!

Our other crewmember, Mike Collins, remained in the command module in lunar orbit. Neil and I got back in our module, lifted off the moon, and rendezvoused with him. All our training with rendezvous had paid off. We returned to Earth safely, fulfilling President Kennedy's goal.

After that, five more Apollo missions landed on the Moon. With the moon goal achieved, could a trip to Mars be next?

NEIL ARMSTRONG SNAPPED THIS PHOTO OF ME ON THE MOON IN JULY 1969.

The Moon

We almost didn't make it to the moon. After the Gemini program in 1966, we prepared to fly the first Apollo test flight. But in 1967, three astronauts were killed in a fire on the launchpad.

The Soviets also suffered a tragedy in 1967. One of their cosmonauts died when his parachute failed during entry. Would either country make it to the moon before 1970?

AFTER OUR RETURN FROM THE MOON, EVERYONE CELEBRATED WITH TICKER-TAPE PARADES.

33

Chapter 3

APPROACHING
MARS

As we move closer to Mars in our cycler, we have a great view out the window. Down below, we see an enormous mountain. This giant is named Olympus Mons after the tallest mountain in Greece, which was the fabled home of the gods. If you put Olympus Mons on Earth, it would cover the state of Arizona, U.S.A.! It would stand three times taller than Mount Everest, the tallest mountain on Earth.

The Race to Mars

Let's hope we don't arrive at Mars during a dust storm! That's what happened to Mariner 9, the first spacecraft to enter Mars orbit, on November 14, 1971. Clouds of dust filled the Martian sky. Only one feature was visible above the clouds: Olympus Mons!

Mariner 9 had arrived just two weeks ahead of the Soviet Mars 2. The Mars 2 completed 362 orbits, and then its lander crashed. The Soviet Mars 3 was the first to make it intact to the surface, but it mysteriously shut down 20 seconds later. It may have been a victim of a dust storm.

Mariner 9 took the first close-up images of Phobos and Deimos. Because these moons of Mars are so small compared to Earth's moon, scientists wondered if they were natural or not. Russian Iosif S. Shklovskii and American Carl Sagan published *Intelligent Life in the Universe* in 1966. These respected astronomers suggested that Phobos and Deimos might be artificial satellites left from an extinct Martian civilization. But the images from Mariner 9 showed Phobos and Deimos to be natural-looking cratered rocks.

Mariner 9 operated until October 1972. After the storm, it provided the first global map of Mars. Carl Sagan had speculated that what Percival Lowell thought were canals were really mid-ocean ridges—only with dust instead of water around them. Mariner 9 showed no ridges. Lowell's canals were only illusions. What Lowell thought were irrigated plants growing along canals were actually dark areas being clouded over and then uncovered by dust storms. But Mariner 9 did reveal a deep canyon that scientists think may have once contained water: the Valles

Marineris (Latin for "Valley of Mariner"). If you put this canyon on Earth, it would stretch all the way across the United States, from California to Washington, D.C.

The next batch of Soviet ships arrived at Mars in February and March of 1974. Mars 4 and 7 missed the planet. Mars 5 failed after a few days in orbit. Mars 6 provided 224 seconds of data—the first data on the

CARL SAGAN DISCUSSES EARTH'S MOON (LEFT). SAGAN STANDS WITH A MODEL OF A VIKING LANDER (RIGHT).

atmosphere of Mars—then crashed. Getting to Mars was a challenge!

The Americans sent two Viking missions in 1976. By this time, Carl Sagan was the best known astronomer in the world. Like Lowell 60 years earlier, Sagan was a science celebrity. He had become a household name in 1973 after appearances on TV. His books about possible alien life were best sellers.

He claimed in the *New York Times* in February 1975 that there is "no reason to exclude from Mars organisms ranging in size from ants to polar bears." As one of the scientists working on the Viking mission, he insisted that the spacecraft include a camera capable of spotting movement. When the Vikings landed, would they see Martian animals?

Viking 1 landed on July 20, 1976, on the desert of Chryse Planitia, which means "plains of gold." No ants or polar bears basked under the pink sky. To check for microbial life, dirt was scooped into onboard biology experiments.

One experiment tried to see if there were any organisms that produced gas. A radioactive broth was added to a sample of soil in a closed chamber. Any organisms present would presumably "drink" the broth and release gas containing radioactive carbon. When the broth was added to the soil, a detector did measure radioactive gas. Was there life on Mars, or had the broth caused a chemical reaction?

Some Mars soil was "cooked" to kill any bacteria present. Broth was added to this sample. As expected, no gas was released. Another sample was warmed enough to kill some bacteria, but not all. When broth was added, some gas was released, though not as much as with the "cold" sample. The scientist in charge, Dr. Gil Levin, said these tests were clear signs that the soil contained microbes. But other scientists insisted that the gas release was still a chemical reaction.

Another Viking experiment seemed to show that there was no life on Mars. All living things we know of have molecules that contain carbon, called organic molecules. This test looked for these molecules. It did not find any.

On September 3, 1976, Viking 2 landed on the Martian "plains of Utopia," Utopia Planitia. The biology experiments produced the same results with soil at this location. Most scientists thought that the organic molecule experiment proved that Mars was lifeless.

However, Dr. Levin suggested that the Viking test for organic molecules may not have been sensitive enough to find Martian bacteria, whereas his gas release experiment was. Because of the amount of radiation, bacteria would not survive on the surface of Mars. So the scoop may have had only a small number of bacteria in it, not enough to show up as organic molecules in the test. The Mars experiments were repeated in Antarctica, where there are very few bacteria on the surface. Just as on Mars, the gas release test indicated bacteria, and the organic molecule test did not.

As for larger creatures, Sagan studied the images from the Viking landers for any sign of animal life, such as snail trails or footprints. All he found was a letter "B" apparently carved into a rock. In a TV appearance, the disappointed Sagan remarked how absurd it would be for aliens to carve the letter B on a rock. The audience roared with laughter.

No Little
Green Men

After the Viking program didn't find life, some people lost interest in Mars. The next American mission wasn't until 1993, and it was an expensive failure. The $813-million-dollar Mars Observer was lost just three days short of reaching Mars. The failure was blamed on a propulsion leak. No one paid much attention to Mars again until 1996.

That summer, news leaked that the August 16, 1996, issue of *Science* magazine would contain a paper offering proof of life on Mars. NASA Administrator Dan Goldin held a press conference. "I want everyone to understand that we are not talking about 'little green men,'" he said about the discovery. "These are extremely small single-cell structures that somewhat resemble bacteria

on Earth." Journalists packed the room to hear more about these microbes. Three NASA scientists described their two-year study of a meteorite from Mars. This 4.5-billion-year-old rock, called ALH84001, had been found in Antarctica. They knew it was from Mars because its chemistry matched that measured by the Viking landers. The scientists claimed to have found structures in the rock similar to fossilized remains of organisms on Earth. They said these were evidence that microscopic bacteria once lived on Mars.

Other scientists said that chemical reactions could explain the structures found in the meteorite. The only way to know for sure was to go to Mars and examine rocks up close.

ALH84001,0

An electron microscope image of ALH84001 shows what look like fossilized bacteria.

Robotic Martian Explorers

Excitement built for a new mission to Mars. The Russians launched Mars 96 in November 1996. The spacecraft fell back to Earth a day later.

The United States' mission, Mars Pathfinder, was ready to go in December of that year. After the expensive failure of Mars Observer, Pathfinder was developed as a "faster, better, cheaper" mission to Mars. The spacecraft and its rover had a budget of only $265 million. On July 4, 1997, it streaked through the Martian night. Explosive bolts ejected a parachute that slowed it down. Three small rockets fired and brought the ship 50 feet (15 m) above the ground. Then, in just one second, four giant airbags made of a bulletproof vest material inflated around the spacecraft. The ball dropped, bounced, and tumbled. It came to rest on the rocky terrain of Ares Vallis. The scientists named the lander the *Carl Sagan Memorial Station*. It opened like a flower. The small rover rolled free to examine nearby rocks. The rover was named Sojourner Truth after an African-American activist who lived during the Civil War.

Pathfinder wasn't designed to check for organic molecules as the Viking landers did. But it revealed hills that had been smoothed by flowing water in the past. It also found a type of rock called quartz. These findings suggested that Mars had been wetter and warmer in the distant past.

Pathfinder quit communicating when its batteries failed in September 1997.

"**Rocks** hold the SECRET TO LIFE'S ORIGINS and history here on Earth and may do the same on remote planets like **MARS.**" —BETHANY EHLMANN, PLANETARY GEOLOGIST

Like I left footprints on the moon, Pathfinder left tracks on Mars.

During this time, the Mars Global Surveyor was supposed to go into orbit around Mars. But a solar panel jammed after launch. Controllers dipped the spacecraft into the Martian atmosphere and used the friction to slow it down, a process called aerobraking. It took several years to ease the spacecraft into orbit around Mars this way. But it worked, and now aerobraking is an accepted way to slow spacecraft down at Mars! This process doesn't use fuel, so it reduces the cost of sending orbiters and cargo to Mars. The Mars Global Surveyor's images proved that Mars had water in the past. Scientists think some of this water is still trapped in the frozen soil.

The next Mars missions, however, were big failures for the United States. In September 1999, the Mars Climate Orbiter crashed. The embarrassing part was the reason why: A program failed to convert English units like feet to metric units like meters. Then, just three months later, twin Mars Polar Landers crashed at the Martian south pole. A software defect told the braking rockets to shut off while the crafts were still 130 feet (40 m) above the surface.

The Japan Aerospace Exploration Agency also failed to reach Mars in 1999. Nozomi (Planet-B) was supposed to arrive in October, but a faulty valve left the spacecraft short of fuel. Japanese engineers swung it around Earth and sent it back to Mars in 2003. But its thrusters broke down. Nozomi never made it to Mars.

NOZOMI

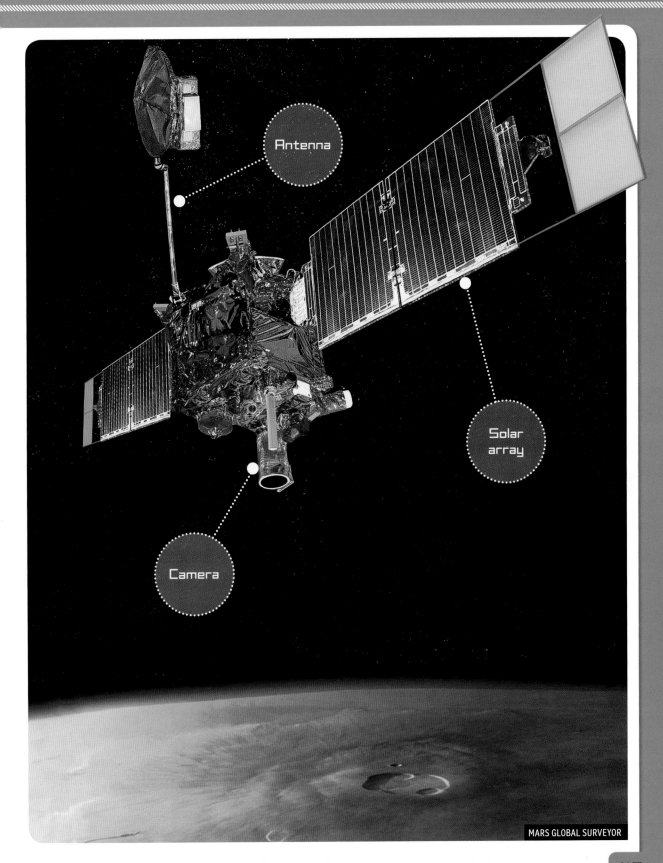

Antenna

Solar array

Camera

MARS GLOBAL SURVEYOR

A New Century
Begins on Mars

NASA sent another orbiter to Mars in 2001. Mars Odyssey got there in October. By 2004, it had mapped the minerals and chemicals on Mars. Mars Odyssey discovered that radiation in Mars orbit is twice as strong as in Earth orbit. Radiation is a form of energy that can be harmful to living things. This information helped engineers design protective shields for our cycler. Odyssey also discovered vast amounts of water ice just below the surface at the poles. This was very good news for those of us wanting to live on Mars!

New plans for sending humans to Mars were announced by U.S. President George W. Bush in January 2004. The Vision for Space Exploration directed NASA to build a new crew exploration vehicle. The new vehicle (named Orion) was supposed to take astronauts to the moon by 2020. "We will then be ready to take the next steps of space exploration: human missions to Mars," President Bush said.

The Europeans were also preparing for future human missions. They'd sent their first orbiter and a lander to Mars in 2003. The lander, called Beagle, crashed. But the Mars Express orbiter began operating in 2004. It is still studying the Martian climate and investigating the moons.

The American Spirit and Opportunity rovers landed on opposite sides of Mars, near the equator, in 2004. Opportunity found evidence that a body of salty water once flowed over its landing area near Eagle crater. Spirit explored a dry plain of volcanic rocks in Gusev crater. It found signs of minerals from ancient water on nearby hills.

Another American orbiter arrived two years later. The Mars Reconnaissance

OPPORTUNITY ROVER

SPIRIT ROVER

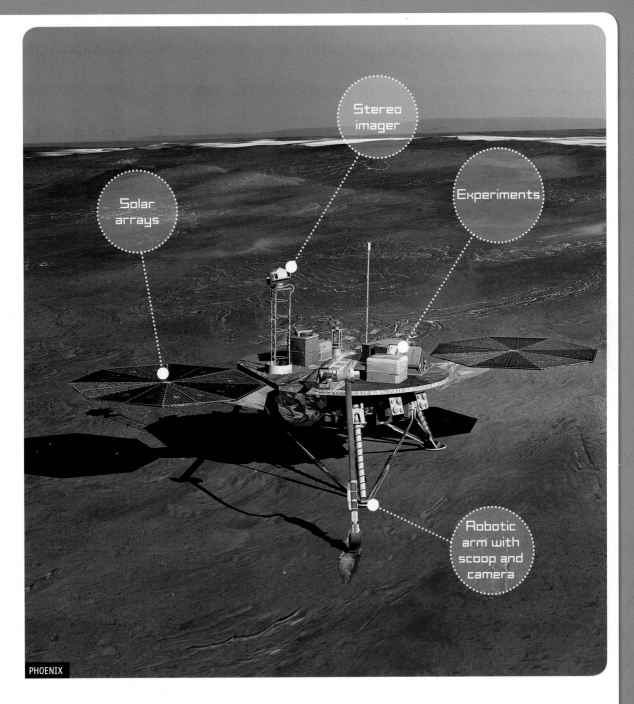

Stereo imager

Solar arrays

Experiments

Robotic arm with scoop and camera

PHOENIX

Orbiter searched for more signs that Mars used to have oceans or seas. Some scientists think the images show an ancient shoreline around the north pole.

One of the most dramatic missions to Mars was the Phoenix lander. This American spacecraft touched down on May 25, 2008.

It landed near the north pole of Mars during the northern summer. Its thrusters exposed ice right below the surface, as predicted by the orbiters. Fascinated scientists watched as the white ice evaporated into the thin Martian air. But as Martian summer ended, Phoenix lost power and quit working.

Political Space

In 2010, I was at Kennedy Space Center with U.S. President Barack Obama. The return-to-the-moon program (called Constellation) was in trouble. A study had shown that without a lot more money, the program wouldn't get to the moon by 2020. The president proposed that NASA stop work on a big new Ares rocket (though Congress kept the program under another name). NASA was to focus on developing technology instead. NASA would also help fund private companies to develop spacecraft to replace the space shuttles and supply the space station. He then added, "By the mid-2030s, I believe we can send humans to orbit Mars and return them safely to Earth."

Other nations were aiming for Mars, too. The Russians launched Phobos-Grunt in 2011, but it failed to leave Earth orbit. The plan had been to land on Phobos and bring back a sample. Also on board was the first Chinese satellite, Yinghuo-1, which was intended to go into Mars orbit.

The biggest rover ever sent to Mars, the American Curiosity, arrived in Gale crater on Mars in August 2012. It is the size of an SUV, and its robotic arm can reach seven feet (2.1 m). The data from Curiosity showed that Mars had had water on the surface for hundreds of millions of years. On Earth, that was enough time for simple forms of life to develop. Understanding what happened to the water as Mars aged is key to finding out if simple life-forms existed or continue to exist on Mars.

If life still exists, it is likely underground where it is safe from radiation and has access to water. In 2013, Curiosity drilled

PRESIDENT BARACK OBAMA AND ME AT KENNEDY SPACE CENTER

DOUGLAS MING TESTS SOIL ON EARTH.

below the surface of Mars to check for signs of life. Soil expert Douglas Ming studied the sample. He found all the elements critical for life including hydrogen, oxygen, carbon, nitrogen, sulfur, and phosphorus. But, as with Lowell a century before, proving life *could* exist does not mean it *did*.

"By the mid-2030s, I believe we can send **humans** to orbit Mars and return them safely to Earth. And a **LANDING ON MARS** will follow. And I expect to be around to see it."

—PRESIDENT BARACK OBAMA

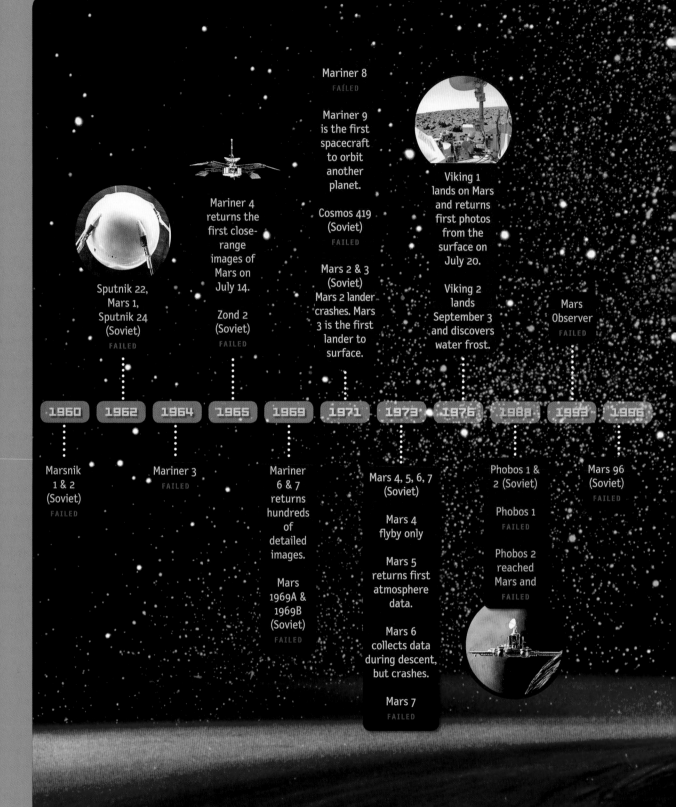

Mariner 8
FAILED

Mariner 9
is the first
spacecraft
to orbit
another
planet.

Cosmos 419
(Soviet)
FAILED

Mars 2 & 3
(Soviet)
Mars 2 lander
crashes. Mars
3 is the first
lander to
surface.

Mariner 4
returns the
first close-
range
images of
Mars on
July 14.

Zond 2
(Soviet)
FAILED

Sputnik 22,
Mars 1,
Sputnik 24
(Soviet)
FAILED

Viking 1
lands on Mars
and returns
first photos
from the
surface on
July 20.

Viking 2
lands
September 3
and discovers
water frost.

Mars
Observer
FAILED

| 1960 | 1962 | 1964 | 1965 | 1969 | 1971 | 1973 | 1976 | 1988 | 1993 | 1996 |

Marsnik
1 & 2
(Soviet)
FAILED

Mariner 3
FAILED

Mariner
6 & 7
returns
hundreds
of
detailed
images.

Mars
1969A &
1969B
(Soviet)
FAILED

Mars 4, 5, 6, 7
(Soviet)

Mars 4
flyby only

Mars 5
returns first
atmosphere
data.

Mars 6
collects data
during descent,
but crashes.

Mars 7
FAILED

Phobos 1 &
2 (Soviet)

Phobos 1
FAILED

Phobos 2
reached
Mars and
FAILED

Mars 96
(Soviet)
FAILED

TIME LINE OF MARS EXPLORATION

Mars Path-
finder lands
on July 4
and deploys
first rover
on Mars.

Mars Global
Surveyor
provides
first alti-
tude maps.
Worked
until 2006.
FAILED

Mars
Climate
Orbiter
FAILED

Mars Polar
Landers
FAILED

Mars Express
(Europe)
Beagle
lander fails,
but orbiter
provides 3-D
color maps.

Mars
Reconnaissance
Orbiter
reveals
seasonal
streaks,
possibly water,
on surface.

Phobos-
Grunt
(Russian)
&
Yinghuo-1
(Chinese)
FAILED

Mangalyaan
Mars Orbiter
(India)
begins study of
Mars surface.

Mars
Atmosphere
and Volatile
EvolutioN
(MAVEN)
begins studying
the
atmosphere.

1997 · 1998 · 1999 · 2001 · 2003 · 2004 · 2006 · 2008 · 2011 · 2012 · 2014

Nozomi
(Japan)
FAILED

Mars Odyssey
maps
Mars water,
heat sources,
and minerals.

Spirit rover
finds
evidence of
ancient water.
Works until
2010.

Opportunity
rover explores
Endeavour
crater.

Phoenix
finds water
at north pole.
Runs out of
power in
November.

Curiosity
explores
Gale crater.
Finds proof
Mars had
deep water
for millions
of years.

MAP OF MARS

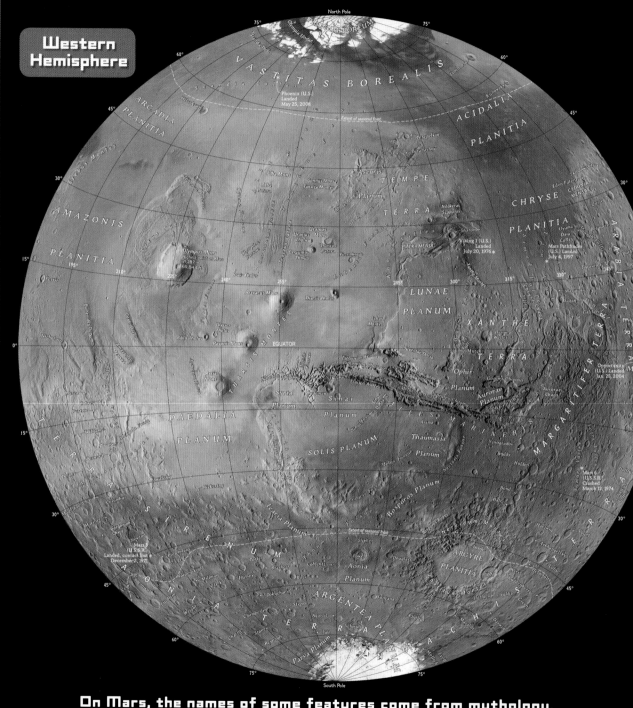

North Pole

75°   75°

60°   60°

45°   45°

30°   30°

15°   15°

0°

VASTITAS BOREALIS

ARCADIA PLANITIA

ACIDALIA PLANITIA

TEMPE TERRA

CHRYSE PLANITIA

AMAZONIS PLANITIA

ARABIA TERRA

LUNAE PLANUM

XANTHE TERRA

EQUATOR

MARGARITIFER TERRA

DAEDALIA PLANUM

SINAI PLANUM

SIRENUM

SOLIS PLANUM

Thaumasia Planum

AONIA PLANUM

ARGYRE PLANITIA

ARGENTEA PLANUM

South Pole

Phoenix (U.S.) Landed May 25, 2008

Viking I (U.S.) Landed July 20, 1976

Mars Pathfinder (U.S.) Landed July 4, 1997

Opportunity (U.S.) Landed Jan. 25, 2004

Mars 6 (U.S.S.R.) Crashed March 12, 1974

Mars 3 (U.S.S.R.) Landed, contact lost December 2, 1971

Olympus Mons highest point on Mars 71,287 ft 69,841 m

On Mars, the names of some features come from mythology.
Other features, like valleys (or *valles* in Latin) bear the name
of the planet in other languages. Big craters are named for
scientists and writers.

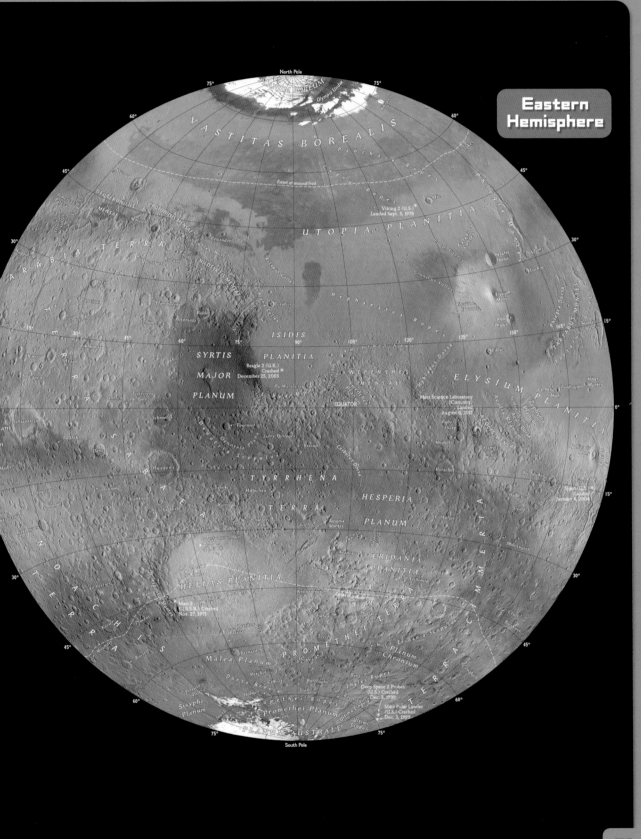

North Pole

75°   75°

60°   60°

O L Y M P I A U N D A E

Olympia Undae

45°   45°

V A S T I T A S   B O R E A L I S

Extent of seasonal frost

30°   30°

Viking 2 (U.S.)
Landed Sept. 3, 1976

U T O P I A   P L A N I T I A

P H L E G R A   M O N T E S

15°

A R A B I A   T E R R A

Renaudot

Hecates
Tholus

T
A
R
T
A
R
U
S

M
O
N
T
E
S

DEUTERONILUS MENSAE

PROTONILUS MENSAE

NILOSYRTIS MENSAE

Elysium
Mons

Albor
Tholus

ISIDIS

SYRTIS
PLANITIA

Beagle 2 (U.K.)

MAJOR   Crashed ★
December 25, 2003

Du Martheray

NEPENTHES
MENSAE

E L Y S I U M

Cerberus Tombaugh

Hibes
Montes

0°

PLANUM

EQUATOR

Mars Science Laboratory
(Curiosity)
Landed
August 6, 2012

P L A N I T I A

0°

Huygens

Fournier

Jarry-Desloges

T E R R A

A
R
A
B
I
A

Schiaparelli

Brazzil

Gale

Sharp

Nicholson

Schroeter

Knobel

15°

S
A
B
A
E
A

T Y R R H E N A

Herschel

Spirit (U.S.) ★
Landed
January 4, 2004

Denning

T E R R A

H E S P E R I A

Millochau

Ausonia
Montes

P L A N U M

Molesworth

N
O
A
C
H
I
S

15°

ERIDANIA
PLANITIA

30°

H E L L A S   P L A N I T I A

Mars 2
(U.S.S.R.) Crashed
Nov. 27, 1971

T E R R A

C I M M E R I A

30°

T E R R A

Barnard

Malea Planum

Mitchel

P R O M E T H E I

T E R R A

Planum
Chronium

45°   45°

Dana

Sisyphi
Planum

Deep Space 2 Probes
(U.S.) Crashed
Dec. 3, 1999

60°   60°

Promethei Planum

Mars Polar Lander
(U.S.) Crashed
Dec. 3, 1999

75°   PLANUM AUSTRALE   75°

South Pole

Chapter 4

RICHES OF MARS

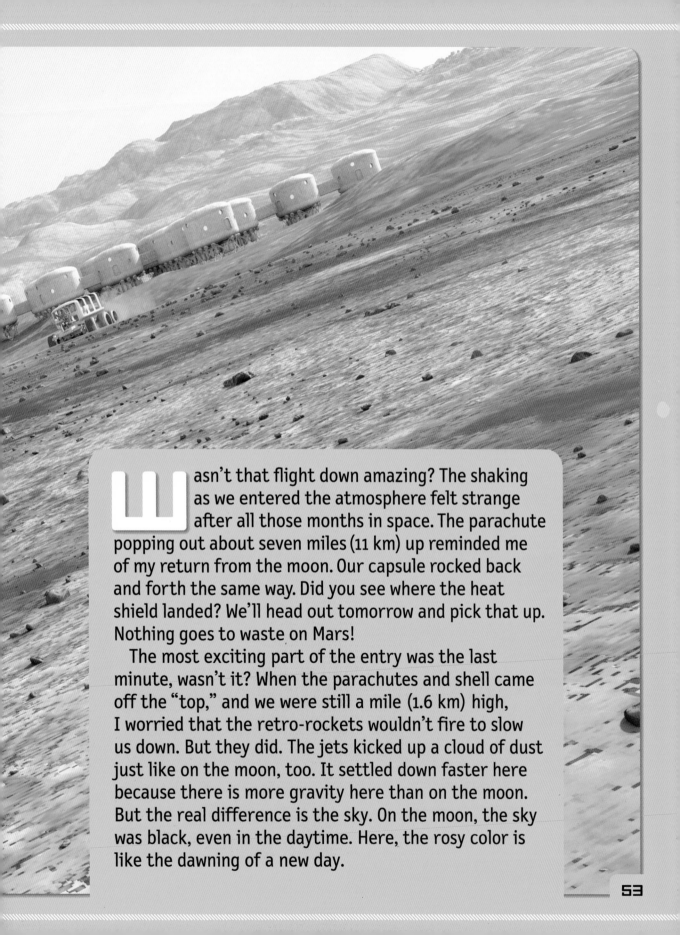

Wasn't that flight down amazing? The shaking as we entered the atmosphere felt strange after all those months in space. The parachute popping out about seven miles (11 km) up reminded me of my return from the moon. Our capsule rocked back and forth the same way. Did you see where the heat shield landed? We'll head out tomorrow and pick that up. Nothing goes to waste on Mars!

The most exciting part of the entry was the last minute, wasn't it? When the parachutes and shell came off the "top," and we were still a mile (1.6 km) high, I worried that the retro-rockets wouldn't fire to slow us down. But they did. The jets kicked up a cloud of dust just like on the moon, too. It settled down faster here because there is more gravity here than on the moon. But the real difference is the sky. On the moon, the sky was black, even in the daytime. Here, the rosy color is like the dawning of a new day.

Welcome to Mars!

After our six-month trip to Mars on the cycler, we will hop into our lander and head down to the surface of Mars. Our Mars landing vehicle will likely be a sort of combination between my Apollo entry capsule and lunar lander—only big enough for six people.

The capsule shape helps slow us down in the atmosphere. The lander's retro-rockets slow us more during the final minute. To protect the rockets, the lander might be placed inside a shell that comes off during entry. The Curiosity rover used a design like that.

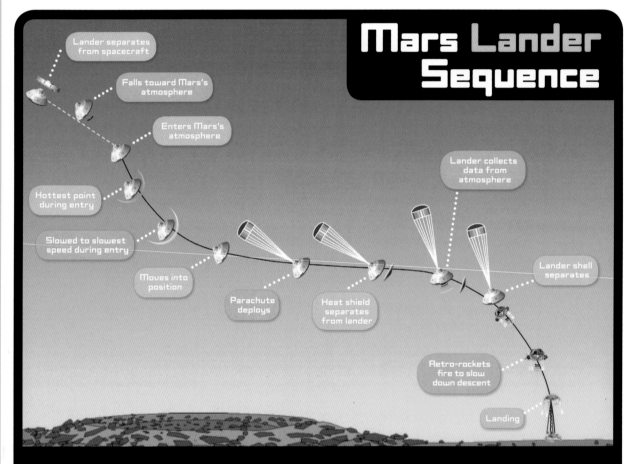

Mars Lander Sequence

- Lander separates from spacecraft
- Falls toward Mars's atmosphere
- Enters Mars's atmosphere
- Hottest point during entry
- Slowed to slowest speed during entry
- Moves into position
- Parachute deploys
- Heat shield separates from lander
- Lander collects data from atmosphere
- Lander shell separates
- Retro-rockets fire to slow down descent
- Landing

LANDING ON MARS will be somewhat different than landing on the moon. For example, unlike the moon, Mars has air. That air will slow us down during entry. That means we can use parachutes to slow down near the surface, like we did returning to Earth from the moon. But the air will also heat up the spacecraft. So we'll need to protect ourselves from the heat.

The Interplanetary Spaceport

The two previous missions identified the best place to put our first spaceport. Our spaceport on Mars won't be like an airport on Earth. Since landers use retro-rockets, we won't need runways. But we'll still need the area to be cleared of big rocks so we don't land on one and tip over!

Flat, rock-free places are hard to find in the southern hemisphere. The land there is pockmarked with craters. But the land in the northern hemisphere is mostly smooth.

Flat areas also tend to be low elevation, and that is good for spacecraft using parachutes to slow down. The lower the elevation, the more air there is above it for the parachutes to use.

The lowest place on Mars is Hellas Basin in the southern hemisphere. But Martian dust storms form near Hellas every Martian year, and sometimes last for months. Dust can ruin pressure seals and damage engines. So we won't be landing there!

The spaceport we're landing at will be located near the Martian equator, near the Valles Marineris canyon system where we will build our first city. Although we plan to stay a long time, if any of us need to go back to Earth, we'll be glad to be near the Martian equator. Launching from near the equator uses less fuel than launching near the poles. To understand why, think about how a pitcher winds up to throw a fastball. The spinning adds speed to the ball's "launch." Likewise, launching from near the equator lets Mars "throw" our spaceships using its natural spin.

THIS TOPOGRAPHICAL MAP SHOWS DIFFERENT ALTITUDES ON MARS. HELLAS BASIN (ARROW) IS ONE OF THE LOWEST POINTS ON MARS.

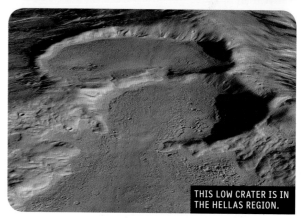

THIS LOW CRATER IS IN THE HELLAS REGION.

Because flights from Earth will arrive in batches every two years, the spaceport won't have a permanent service center or staff. Instead, we'll probably tow our lander to a hangar for storage. (It needs protection from radiation and dust.) Or, we might just cover it with the used parachutes until it's refitted for use as an ascent vehicle or needed for spare parts.

The Arrival!

We park our rover in the temporary garage and step into the "dust room" before entering the air lock. We need to remove the dust that sticks to our suits. The rusty dust on Mars has iron in it. Iron sticks to magnets. So we use magnetic brushes to pull most of the dust off our suits. After a good dusting, we step into the air lock and run a vacuum over our boots to get any pebbles that are stuck in the treads or folds. Then we pump in the air. We take off our helmets and suck in our first lungful of Martian air. Does it smell a little rusty to you?

Our fellow pioneers greet us as we come out of the air lock. We hook up our space suits to the battery chargers, take our two-minute showers, and dress in coveralls. Our hosts take our photos to share on the news back on Earth. Even though we haven't picked a place to build our home yet, we're already famous just for being here!

They then take us to a large meeting room that also serves as a cafeteria. It has a microwave and a water spigot and an old oxygen tank to serve as a sink. We sit at tables and settle on stools made of old cargo containers, each one different. One crewmember jokes that this place will someday be either the first Martian spaceport museum or the first Martian restaurant!

We celebrate our arrival with a special meal, including some sweet potato pie made from yams grown in a rack here on Mars. Until we get our permanent greenhouse built, we'll be stuck eating mostly packets of food sent from Earth on cargo flights. But we hope to find a place soon somewhere in or near the Valles Marineris canyon that has all the resources we need to build our permanent home.

THE FIRST CREWS WILL REUSE EVERYTHING, INCLUDING MAKING FURNITURE!

THIS VALLEY LEADING TOWARD VALLES MARINERIS LIKELY ONCE HELD RUNNING WATER.

Mars Resources

What resources do we need to live here permanently? Take a deep breath. People need air to breathe! And that's just the start. We also need water, food, and materials to make clothes and everything else. Our houses on Mars will need to shelter us not just from the cold and lack of air outside, but also from radiation. We'll need power to run the lights, fans, and computers. To stay in touch with our friends on Earth, we'll also need communications. To get around, we'll need transportation, and fuel. Where can we get these things on Mars?

Mars is half the size of Earth in diameter, but none of its surface is covered by oceans. So the land area of Mars is about the same as that of Earth. We could probably survive just about anywhere on Mars, but, like on Earth, some places will have easier access to the resources we need.

Space Suits

All of us will arrive on Mars wearing our space suits. The suits will protect us in case of a cabin leak. For safety reasons, we probably won't land very close to our temporary homes. So we'll either ride in a "dune buggy" we bring with us like on the last three Apollo flights, or we'll drive there in a pressurized rover. We'll need a pressurized rover for exploring long distances.

Our Mars suits will be different from the ones we used in space. In space, we were weightless, and so were our suits. We didn't worry about sore feet or bending and stooping. But as I discovered on the moon, carrying a heavy suit around on the ground is tiring. Our new Mars suits will be light and flexible. But if we have to walk a long ways outside, we'll get a robotic luggage cart.

And though our suits come equipped with diapers, I'm sure we'll be anxious to get indoors and use a bathroom!

SCIENTISTS TEST THE FLEXIBLE NEW SPACE SUIT IN A WIND TUNNEL.

HERE I AM WITH SPACE SUIT DESIGNER DAVA NEWMAN. WE'RE POSING WITH THE MARS SPACE SUIT SHE DESIGNED.

Red Planet Recreation

Mars has another resource you may not have thought about—natural entertainment! Getting around on the surface of Mars offers lots of challenges, but also opportunities. Dirt bikes and zip lines may offer practical, and exciting, ways of crossing rough ground and deep canyons. Pioneers may sled the frozen north and south poles on robotically pulled dogsleds. Giant airships might lift people and gear high into the sky above towering mountains.

Here, the tallest volcano and the deepest valleys in the solar system are sure to lure people to climb and cross them in a variety of ways. Prizes might entice people to invent ways to cross Hellas Basin, or climb into and out of the caldera of Olympus Mons in the shortest time. The low gravity, freezing temperatures, and lack of air will require creative new designs, and will surely lead to some new sports.

Snowboarding or bobsledding may be especially popular on Mars in the spring. Mars's surface is streaked with long furrows called gullies that are about four to seven feet (1 to 2 m) across. Scientists think these gullies were caused by dry ice melting and cutting channels downhill.

To prove their theory, scientists took a block of dry ice from a supermarket and sat it on top of a sand dune in Utah. They sat a block of water ice beside it. As the day warmed, the water ice melted and soaked into the sand. But the dry ice formed a layer of gas underneath. It slid down the sand dune, leaving a track like the gullies on Mars. Imagine skiing down a gully like that!

ACTIVITY: MEET EARTH'S LITTLE BROTHER

Earth is definitely bigger than Mars. But how much bigger? It depends on how you compare them! Do this activity to compare the sizes of Earth and Mars three different ways.

SUPPLIES

- Piece of paper
- Ruler or geometric compass
- Pencil
- Blue and red colored pencils
- Half cup of blue modeling clay
- Half cup of red modeling clay
- Tablespoon
- Cutting board
  [or wax paper for
  on top of table/desk]
- Plastic knife
- 11 pennies

COMPARE EARTH AND MARS
BY DIAMETER [Width]

1 With a ruler, draw a line 4 inches (10 cm) long on the paper and mark it at every inch (2.5 cm).

2 Make a circle 2 inches (5 cm) in diameter (with the center at the 1-inch [2.5-cm] mark). Label this circle "Mars." Color it red.

3 Make a 4-inch circle surrounding the smaller one (with the center on the 2-inch mark). This is Earth. Color it blue. Earth is twice as big (by diameter) as Mars!

COMPARE EARTH AND MARS
BY VOLUME [Space]

1 Fill 1 tablespoon (15 ml) with red clay.

2 On a cutting board or wax paper, roll the clay into a "Mars" ball.

3 Measure out 6 tablespoons (90 ml) of blue clay.

4 Roll the 6 spoonfuls into an "Earth" ball. Earth is six times bigger (by volume) than Mars!

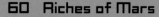

COMPARE EARTH AND MARS
BY MASS [Weight]

1 Place the Earth and Mars clay balls on a cutting board.

2 Use a plastic knife to cut Mars almost in half.

3 Place one penny inside and roll it back into a ball.

4 Then use the knife to cut Earth almost in half.

5 Place ten pennies in the cut and roll it back into a ball.

6 Hold Mars in one hand and Earth in the other. Earth is ten times bigger (by mass) than Mars!

THE FACTS

MASS	0.10 Earth Mass, 7×10^{20} tons
DIAMETER	0.53 Earth Diameter, 4,221 miles (6,792 km)
GRAVITY	0.37 Earth gravity, 12.1 feet/second^2 (3.7 m/s^2)
LENGTH OF DAY (SOL)	24 hours 39 minutes
DISTANCE FROM SUN	1.5 AU*
DISTANCE FROM EARTH	0.5 to 2.0 AU
LENGTH OF YEAR	687 Earth days
AXIAL TILT	25.2 degrees

MAGNETIC FIELD	no
SURFACE PRESSURE	0.01 atmosphere (1/100th of sea level on Earth)
TEMPERATURE	-67°F (-55°C) average, but varies from -207°F (-133°C) at the poles in winter to 80°F (27°C) near the equator in summer
GASES IN AIR	carbon dioxide (95%), nitrogen (3%), argon (1%); less than 1%: oxygen and other gases

*1 AU is Earth distance from sun, 93 million miles (149 million km)

Mars Gas

You can't breathe the air on Mars. It is too thin, and it is mostly a gas called carbon dioxide that people exhale. Mars also has about 3 percent nitrogen, 1 percent argon, and less than 1 percent of oxygen, water vapor, and other gases in its atmosphere.

People need oxygen to breathe, burn fuel, and use in batteries. How do we get it on Mars? Water is made out of hydrogen and oxygen. So we can melt ice we find on Mars and use electricity to get the oxygen out of it.

Though people can breathe pure oxygen, it is not safe to live in a pure-oxygen environment because of the danger of fires.

Something that would not catch fire in normal air, like steel wool, will burn easily in pure oxygen. The only time we use pure oxygen to breathe is inside our space suits where there is little danger of fire.

The air on Earth is about 20 percent oxygen and 80 percent nitrogen. Nitrogen is a colorless, odorless gas that doesn't hurt people, and nitrogen reduces the danger of fires. We could filter nitrogen out of the air already in Mars's atmosphere and pump it into our habitat to mix with the oxygen so it's like Earth. Or we might get it by melting rocks that contain nitrogen.

Argon is a colorless, odorless gas like

UNLIKE ON EARTH, THE AIR ON MARS IS MOSTLY CARBON DIOXIDE.

nitrogen that also is harmless for people to breathe. Mars has argon in its atmosphere. So if nitrogen is scarce, we can use argon to dilute the oxygen and reduce our fire risk.

Once we have our greenhouses going, we'll probably get most of our oxygen on Mars the way we do on Earth: from plants. Plants absorb carbon dioxide, which we can pump into a greenhouse from the Martian air. The plants then "exhale" oxygen that we can use in our habs.

CURIOSITY TOOK THIS IMAGE OF AN ANCIENT STREAMBED. MARS PIONEERS COULD EXTRACT WATER FROM THE SOIL HERE.

"When you have a brand-new **problem,** you need as many TOOLS AS YOU CAN GET."
—CONSTANCE ADAMS, SPACE ARCHITECT

Spirit on Husband Hill in Gusev crater

Powerful Sun

We definitely need energy to live, and most of that energy comes from the sun. Because Mars is farther from the sun than Earth is, the sun is not as bright on Mars as it is on Earth. To human eyes, it is about as bright as it is on Earth while wearing sunglasses. But there are no rainy days on Mars! So except for seasonal dust storms, there is plenty of sunlight to turn into electricity using solar cells. Focused sunlight (using mirrors or lenses) can also be used to boil water and run turbine engines for power.

The length of a Martian day, called a sol, is 24 hours, 39 minutes, and 35 seconds. But the amount of daylight depends on the season. Mars has four seasons in the same order as Earth: spring, summer, fall, and winter. Just like on Earth, the seasons are caused by the tilt of Mars's axis to the sun. But because Mars takes about twice as long to go around the sun as Earth takes, the seasons last about twice as long on Mars. Also, like Earth, except for a band around the equator, daytime is shorter in winter than in summer. Close to the poles, the sun doesn't even make it above the horizon in winter! If we build near the poles, we can't depend on sunshine for power. Luckily, Valles Marineris is near the equator, so it should have plenty of sunshine for us in all seasons.

The brightness of sunlight also changes as Mars goes around in its orbit. Unlike Earth's nearly circular orbit, Mars's is more like an oval. When Mars is closest to the sun, the light is about 20 percent brighter than when it is farthest away. Mars is closer to the sun when it is summer in the southern hemisphere and winter in the north. This

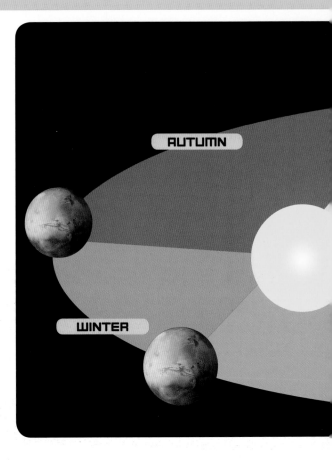

brighter sunlight makes the southern summer warmer (though it is still freezing!), and the northern winter not as cold as southern winter. Brighter sunlight also produces more electricity. But again, if we build near the equator, we will have the most sunshine that is available no matter where Mars is in its orbit.

The light on Mars may be dimmer, but it has enough ultraviolet light to kill plants. This light is mostly blocked by the atmosphere on Earth. The atmosphere of Mars is too thin to stop these harmful rays. So windows used for greenhouses or buildings for other living things will need to be coated to block this light. The best coatings currently available are made out of gold and silver, so they will probably be imported from Earth.

SEASONS IN
THE NORTHERN HEMISPHERE

SUMMER

SPRING

MARS HAS FOUR SEASONS, SHOWN HERE
FOR THE NORTHERN HEMISPHERE.

THE AVERAGE POWER USED PER HOME IN THE UNITED STATES IS
ABOUT 1 KILOWATT PER HOUR. IF THE PANELS SHOWN HERE ARE 5
FEET (1.5 M) TALL AND 4 FEET (1.2 M) WIDE, IT WOULD TAKE ABOUT
10 ROWS OF 12 PANELS TO MAKE THAT MUCH POWER ON MARS.

ACTIVITY: PASS THE LIGHT, PLEASE

Martian habitats will likely be in caves or buried under dirt to protect people from radiation. But they won't have to live in the dark! Light travels in a straight line. When it strikes something black, it is "soaked up." [That's why black things get so hot in the sun!] Light bounces, or reflects, off mirrors and white things, sending the light in a straight line in a new direction. Try this activity to see how Mars settlers might use wall hangings to light up or darken their rooms.

SUPPLIES

- Closet or bathroom with no windows
- Small flashlight with a wide beam, such as a cell phone flashlight
- 12-inch ruler or meter stick
- Three cereal boxes [do not have to be empty!] about 1 foot [30 cm] tall
- Tape
- One small mirror
- Two pieces of white unlined paper
- Two pieces of black unlined paper
- Small light-colored toy figure with markings

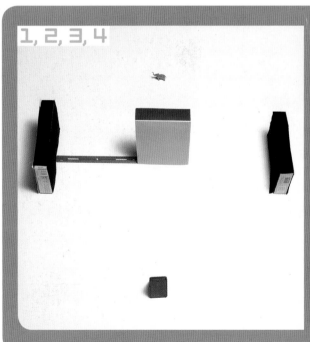

1, 2, 3, 4

5

DIRECTIONS

1 Leave one cereal box plain. Tape a sheet of white paper to one side of each of the other two boxes. Tape a sheet of black paper to the other side of these two boxes.

2 Clear a place on the floor in a closet (or window-less room) about 2 by 2 feet (0.4 m²). Place the flashlight on the floor. Lay the ruler in front of it. Sit the plain box at the distance of the ruler from the flashlight.

3 Place the toy on the opposite side of the box from the flashlight, about the same distance away. The toy will be in the shadow of the box, blocked from the light, like a person inside a room with no windows.

4 Place the two boxes with the black side facing the flashlight 1 foot (30 cm) on either side of the plain box. Rotate them so they face each other with the plain box between them.

5 Turn on the flashlight. Turn off all other lights. The toy should be hidden in the shadow of the plain box. Can you see any markings or colors on the toy?

6 Flip the side boxes around so the white sides are facing each other. Can you see markings or colors on the toy now?

7 Place the mirror against the white side of one of the side boxes. Tilt it until it bounces the flashlight light onto the toy. Is it much better than the white paper?

8 Turn on the overhead light or open the door. Note the color of the walls in the closet or bathroom. Did some light bounce off the walls and change the brightness of the toy?

DURING A RAGING DUST STORM LIKE THIS ONE, WIND MOVES QUICKLY.

Dust Storms

Remember I told you the lowest place on Mars is Hellas Basin and that's where dust storms start? Like hurricanes on Earth that usually form in the ocean in the summer and fall, dust storms on Mars are also tied to the season. Storms usually begin near Hellas Basin during southern spring as Mars gets closer to the sun. The storms start there because Hellas is the deepest (3.7 mi/6 km) basin on the planet. The air at the bottom is warmer by about 20°F (11°C) than at the top. The warm air rises and takes dust with it. A storm in 1971 lasted a month, and one in 2001 lasted three months. Both covered the entire planet. Even during dust storms, enough sunlight gets through to produce some power. To be safe, though, we will want batteries or other power sources to use during storms.

We might generate power from the storm itself! Because the air is so thin, dust storms are the only time the wind blows fast enough (100 ft/s, 30 m/s) to operate a wind turbine. The best locations for capturing this seasonal power source will be atop high mountains. If we build in the Valles Marineris, we might put a turbine up on the southern rim.

Dust-Free Power

Another option for power during dust storms, and any other time, is nuclear power. Nuclear reactors could be built out of Martian materials. But nuclear fuel is rare and dangerous. Even if enough of it is located on Mars, it requires special processing. Nuclear reactors and their fuel do last a long time, though. So it may make sense to import this source of power from Earth.

Geothermal power may be the best long-term power source available on Mars. Scientists don't yet know where the best "hot spots" are, but they are likely to be near volcanoes. Volcanoes don't need to be active to have hot magma inside them. Even volcanoes that erupted millions of years ago may still have hot magma pockets. The hot

magma may have melted ice and created deep wells full of liquid water.

Both the underground heat and any wells can be used to produce power. First, we'd have to drill down to the heat source. If there is water there, it might gush up like a geyser! But if there isn't water, we can pour some down the hole. The heat then boils the water. The rising steam turns a turbine to create electricity. The steam is cooled back into water and sent down to be heated again. On Earth, Iceland gets most of its power from using this clean, renewable source. Because power is so vital to life on Mars, finding one of these geothermal hot spots will be a priority during our exploration of the canyons.

THIS GEOTHERMAL POWER STATION PROVIDES POWER IN ICELAND.

Ice Water

Spacecraft have found plenty of evidence that Mars once had rivers, lakes, and maybe even oceans in the distant past. But Mars is too cold to have liquid water on the surface now. What is harder to understand is why ice is only seen at or near the poles. On Earth, air pressure helps hold water and ice on the surface. But even so, water evaporates easily into the air. As it rises, it gets cooler and forms clouds. When the clouds are thick enough, they produce rain or snow.

It never rains or snows on Mars. Any ice exposed to the air evaporates. Clouds do form, but they never get thick enough to make snow. And it's too cold for rain. The evaporated ice finds its way back down to the surface as frost. Most of the frost forms near the poles.

But there is plenty of ice mixed into Martian soil. Even near the equator, the Curiosity rover found ice in the dirt. Heating that dirt forces the water out of it. About three cubic feet (0.08 m³) of dirt would produce six pints (2.8 L) of water, enough for one person for a day. Dirt deeper under the surface likely has even more water frozen in it. Scientists predict that the ice-rich layer may be miles thick in some places.

VIKING IMAGE SHOWING POLAR ICE

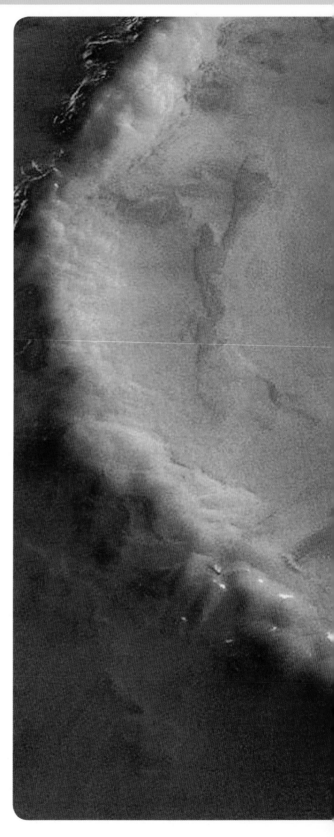

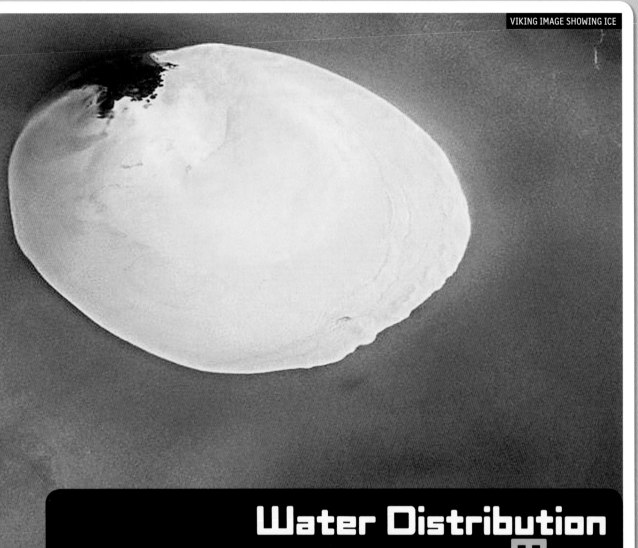

Water Distribution on Mars

The poles of Mars are the wettest [dark blue and purple], and the craters, such as Hellas Basin, are the driest [tan and white].

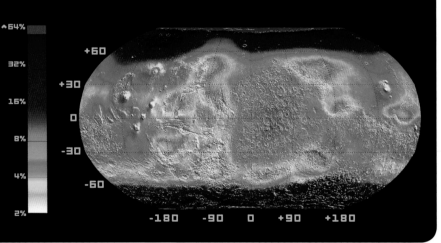

64%
32%
16%
8%
4%
2%

+60
+30
0
-30
-60

-180 -90 0 +90 +180

ACTIVITY: MAKING SWISS CHEESE TERRAIN

The poles on Mars have two kinds of ice: regular water ice like on Earth, and carbon dioxide ice called dry ice. Instead of melting like water ice on Earth, dry ice goes from solid to gas. As pockets of dry ice "boil" out of the ground, the surface sinks. Small pits become larger over time and sometimes merge into each other. Do this activity to see how warming up the Martian south pole leads to some rather funny-looking "Swiss cheese" terrain!

SUPPLIES

- Flour
- Water
- Tablespoon
- Butter knife
- Cereal bowl, microwave safe
- Microwave
- Oven mitts
- Two pieces of black unlined paper
- Marshmallows [mini preferred]

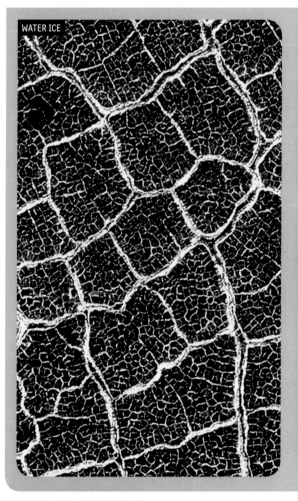

WATER ICE

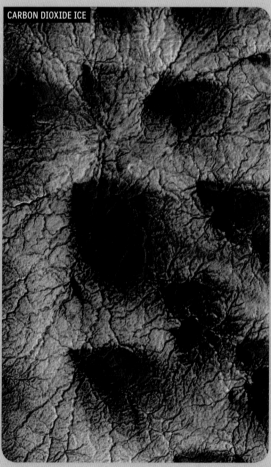

CARBON DIOXIDE ICE

DIRECTIONS

1 Measure 8 tablespoons (120 ml) of flour into a microwave-safe cereal bowl. Add about 8 tablespoons water and stir using the butter knife until it is a smooth dough.

2 Add about a dozen mini marshmallows (or cut up large marshmallows with scissors). Stir with knife until they are covered up by the dough. Smooth over the surface with the knife and run it around the edge of the bowl to make it look like a pancake. (If it has too much water to hold that shape, mix in a little more flour.)

3 Place bowl in the microwave on high for 2 minutes. Watch through the window as the marshmallows puff up out of the flour and boil away. As the dry ice on Mars is heated by the sun in summer, it "puffs" up out of the ground, too, turning from a solid to a gas.

4 Open the microwave door. Be careful! The bowl and marshmallows will be hot! Use oven mitts to remove the bowl. Note that the heated marshmallows have left holes in the flour "terrain" just like carbon dioxide leaves pits in the Martian south pole. Does it look like Swiss cheese to you?!

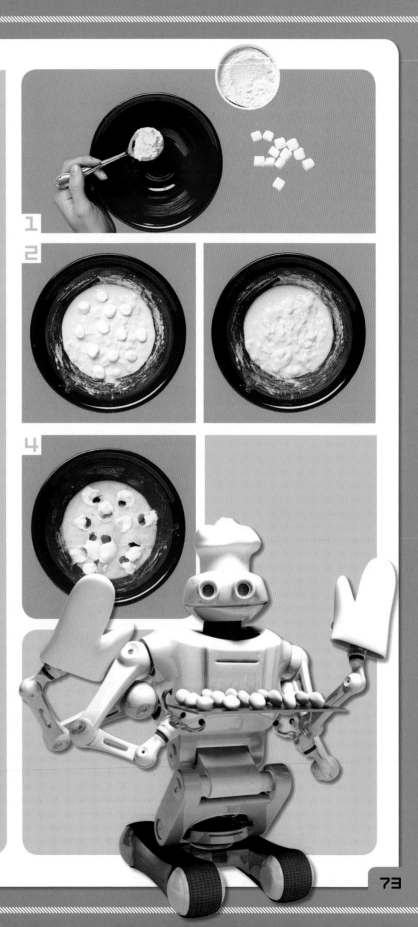

73

Under Pressure

Whee-oo, whee-oo! That's the air alarm! Grab your emergency gear and head to the nearest air lock. Don your space suit and then help your buddy.

Did you and your buddy get suited in less than ten minutes? No? Then you need more drills! Your lives depend on your quick response.

To put it bluntly, the surface of Mars is deadly. An unprotected person would die in minutes. There's no air to breathe, and you can't even hold your breath. The air is literally sucked out of you by the low pressure outside. Your eyes would bug out, your eardrums would burst, you'd wet your pants, and whatever you had for lunch would explode out of your mouth and nose. Your body would end up freeze-dried. But none of us are going to die that way. We practice emergency drills regularly, like fire drills at school, so we know what to do.

Though living on Mars has its dangers, the home we're building may be safer than many on Earth. After all, we don't have to worry about hurricanes, tornadoes, lightning, earthquakes, or floods. And we know how to deal with low pressure from years of experience on the International Space Station.

Besides having space suits to protect us, each room is a separate module, like on the space station. If there's a fire or a leak in any module, it can be sealed off from the rest. Also like on the space station, each module has an emergency air supply. This supply gives us time to escape. Fire and contamination are always a concern, but leaks are rare because our homes are buried under lots of dirt.

THICK AIR COLLECTS AT THE BOTTOM OF DEEP CANYONS AND CONDENSES INTO CLOUDS AND FROST.

ACTIVITY: PRESSURE AROUND THE HOUSE?

On Earth, the air inside a house pushes out the same amount as the air outside pushes in. But on Mars, there is almost no air outside. So the air inside the house pushes against the walls to get out. Air pushing on corners makes them bow outward and even break. Cylinders and spheres don't have this problem. Do this activity to see for yourself why homes on Mars will be round.

SUPPLIES

- Letter or card envelope
- Scissors
- Tape
- 12-inch (30-cm) balloon

DIRECTIONS

1. Cut off the bottom half inch (13 mm) of a standard envelope. (It will be two layers thick with the fold at the bottom.) Discard the rest of the envelope.

2. Cut the ends off so the remaining strip is about 6 inches (15 cm) long.

3. Place one end inside the other to make a loop. Secure it with a wrap of tape.

4. Pinch and crease the loop in four places to make it a rectangle or square. This is like a rectangular house on Earth.

5. Fill the balloon with air to pre-stretch it. Then let the air out.

6. Place the deflated balloon through the paper rectangle with some of the end sticking out the other side.

7. Blow up the balloon. What happens to the rectangular shape?

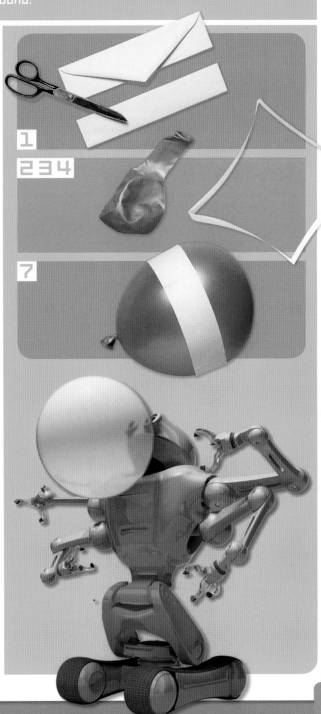

Shields Up!

People and plants need energy to live. But too much, in the form of radiation, can be harmful. Radiation comes from the sun and stars in the form of light and particles called cosmic rays. Harmful light is blocked by shades and filters. But cosmic rays can burn right through the metal hulls of spacecraft and modules.

When our team left for Mars, we packed food and water around the outer walls of our spacecraft to soak up most of this radiation. Scientists are developing a magnetic shield that may work even better. But unless we get a big dose of radiation all at once, radiation won't kill us. The reason it is dangerous is that it can damage cells inside our body and cause cancer later. But the dose we get, even on a round-trip to Mars, increases our risk of cancer only about 3 percent.

Fortunately, on Mars, we can stop these atomic "bullets" by burying our habitats. Under 16 feet (5 m) of dirt, we'll get the same amount of radiation we get on the surface of Earth.

Moving all the dirt is a lot of work! So we might move into a cave or a natural underground tunnel called a lava tube. Orbiting spacecraft have already spotted a few of these. Caves also have the advantage of holding a steady temperature day and night. The average temperature on Mars ranges from about -190°F (-123°C) to about 70°F (21°C). It can vary by more than 100°F (54°C) in one sol. Equipment lasts longer when it's kept at a steady temperature, even if that temperature is below freezing.

If there aren't any good caves, we can create our own! We could inflate a giant plastic bubble in a crater, fill the bottom with dirt to hold it down, and then cover the top with dirt. Or we can build a brick dome next to a cliff. Because the gravity of Mars is about a third of Earth's, the bricks won't weigh as much as they would on Earth. A pressurized plastic or glass dome should be able to support the dirt even without pillars to hold up the roof. But we might want pillars anyway, just because they look cool!

Metal Mars

Iron, aluminum, and silicon are very important to the construction of our homes on Mars. Luckily for us, all three of these elements are easy to find everywhere on the surface of Mars.

Tiny rusted iron particles are why dust on Mars is red and the sky is pink. Because iron is a soft metal, people usually mix it with carbon to make steel. We can get carbon from the Martian air and rocks. Steel is strong and resistant to acids. It's a good choice for pressure containers.

Aluminum is a very useful metal. It doesn't rust, is very lightweight, and is easy to work with. We use it for making everything from forks to spacecraft. Unfortunately, it takes a lot of power to get it out of the rock. Because power will be expensive on Mars, instead of using aluminum for things like soda cans, people may use glass instead.

Glass is made from silicon, the main ingredient of beach sand. Silicon is the most common element in the Martian crust. So we'll have plenty of silicon to make solar cells,

glass jars, and greenhouse windows. We might even use it to make glass roads by rolling a hot cylinder over the ground!

Other metals, such as copper, nickel, zinc, silver, and gold, may be rare on Mars. During planet formation, most of these dense metals sank below the surface where they mixed and melted. This melted rock, called magma, erupted as lava from volcanoes. When the lava encountered air and water, it formed minerals that include these metals. When Mars was warmer, some of these minerals may have been carried into nearby streams. So we might find these metals in Valles Marineris "downstream" from the big volcanoes.

Another place we might find metals on Mars is in the mountains surrounding big impact craters, called basins, where large space rocks hit Mars's surface. Large impacts produce volcanic activity by heating, thinning, and cracking the crust. So three large impact sites, Hellas, Argyre, and Isidis, may be good places to find rare metals.

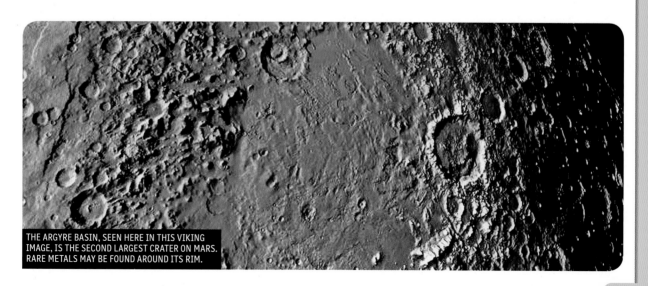

THE ARGYRE BASIN, SEEN HERE IN THIS VIKING IMAGE, IS THE SECOND LARGEST CRATER ON MARS. RARE METALS MAY BE FOUND AROUND ITS RIM.

EARLY GREENHOUSES ON MARS MAY GROW PLANTS IN SOIL OR WATER WITH NUTRIENTS FROM EARTH, OR LATER SUPPLIED BY ROCKS FOUND ON MARS.

Growing Nutrients on Mars

To stay on Mars, we have to grow our own food. Luckily, Mars has everything but the seeds, which we have brought with us from Earth. We may grow these in water or soil, but either way, we have to make sure the plants get the light and nutrients they need.

Nutrients are elements needed for life and growth. Plants need 16 nutrients. Plants absorb three of these (carbon, oxygen, and hydrogen) through air and water. Soil is the usual source for the others.

The most important soil nutrients are nitrogen, phosphorus, potassium, calcium, magnesium, and sulfur. These elements are not found in pure forms on Earth or Mars. They are mixed up in rocks that get crushed or cracked to make soil.

Scientists don't yet know how much of

Hydroponics is a method of growing plants in nutrient-rich water instead of soil.

THESE BEAN PLANTS ARE BEING GROWN IN A LABORATORY WITH THE HELP OF ADDED PLANT HORMONES THAT MAKE THE PLANTS GROW BETTER IN THEIR ENVIRONMENT.

each nutrient is available in rocks at specific locations on Mars. But rovers have found at least some of all the important nutrients. Spirit, which landed near the equator, found rocks containing phosphorus, potassium, calcium, and magnesium. Curiosity found some of these elements as well as nitrogen and sulfur.

Plants and people also need metals to stay healthy. These metals include iron, magnesium, manganese, copper, and zinc. All of these have been found in rocks on Mars.

CURIOSITY DROVE OVER THIS ROCK IN 2013 AND BROKE IT, REVEALING ITS BLUISH INTERIOR. IT CONTAINS ALL THE NUTRIENTS PLANTS NEED TO SURVIVE.

Chapter 5

MARTIAN HOME

Moving Day!

After months of exploring, we've found the perfect place to build our first permanent Martian home. We decided to use a recent crater that is near a geothermal hot spot. We set up a giant solar-powered oven to bake the water and metals we need out of the soil. Our handyman robots made tons of bricks for us, and our 3-D printers pressed out all the glass and plastics we need for our greenhouses. We imported some inflatable domes from Earth that arrived at our spaceport via cargo ships.

It took us years to finish the first ring of modules and put the dome over the top. The work went faster after another set of crewmembers arrived on the cycler. We were all really tired of commuting back and forth to the spaceport! We're going to name that road after the person who made the most trips—was that you?!

Finally the first settlers, 18 of us, are ready to move into the Founders Dome!

After we exit the air lock, our group splits up and heads for the men's or women's suit rooms. We hook up our space suits to the battery chargers, take our two-minute showers (some things never change!), and dress in whatever cultural styles we prefer. Smile for the cameras! We're making a video tour for the folks back on Earth.

As we walk through the storage tunnel to the settlement, you show the folks back on Earth the skylights we installed to keep power usage down. You also show them the spider and closet plants growing in planters along the walls. Not only are these plants lovely, but they also don't need much light or water. They produce oxygen and scrub toxins from the air, too. No wonder it smells so fresh in here!

SPIDER PLANTS LIKE THESE CAN PROVIDE OXYGEN INDOORS.

MARS FOR SALE

When we landed on the moon in 1969, we planted an American flag. But we didn't claim the moon for the United States. Instead, we brought a plaque with us that said we came in peace for all mankind.

The United States, the Soviet Union, and other nations of the world signed a treaty in 1967 to govern our behavior in space. The signers agreed that they would not place weapons in space. They also agreed not to claim the moon, Mars, or other worlds as their territory. The language of the treaty left open the possibility for individuals or companies to claim land, though. They could then develop their property at their own expense. Another treaty, called the Moon Treaty, would prevent this, too. But the United States and the Soviet Union never signed it.

Will the nations of the world still honor the 1967 treaty when they get to Mars? Will private companies or individuals claim property and develop it? How big an area can they claim? Do they have to live on the land, or can they mine it with robots? Space lawyers will need to address these issues in the near future to avoid conflicts over who owns what.

Another issue is who will pay for preserving or protecting historical places, such as the place where people first land on Mars. Will the first landing place be a historical monument that anyone can visit? As one of the founding pioneers of Mars, maybe you will run the museum that contains the space suit you wore when you arrived!

WELCOME TO YOUR NEW BEDROOM. HANG YOUR CLOTHES IN THE CLOSET, THEN CHOOSE A VIEW TO LOOK OUT YOUR "WINDOW."

Our new home is not that different from a five-star hotel with an atrium in the center and skylight above. The first floor has a lobby with places to sit and socialize, plus work rooms, labs, and shops. After a hard sol's work, a swim in the lake is very refreshing. Just watch out for the fish!

Our cafeteria here is much nicer than the Spaceport Kitchen. This one serves two meals a day, breakfast and dinner. Everyone takes a sack lunch to work or snacks they can eat in their space suits. No one is allowed to cook in their room. We learned on Earth in Antarctica that it is safer to have all cooking done in one central place rather than risk fires in the rooms. It is also more efficient to cook for groups of people than for one person at a time. Besides, we all enjoy eating together.

Let's show the Earth folks our bedrooms (while they are still neat and tidy!). They're on the upper deck, or floor. They are like hotel rooms except that there is only one bathroom per floor, like at school. Having the plumbing centralized makes it easier to recycle our water and waste. There is no elevator. In the low gravity, no one minds a few stairs, though. We also have a flat spiraling track beside the stairs that runners and robots use. There are rumors that the round outer wall is good for skateboarding, but I wouldn't know about that.

We climb the stairs to the upper deck. We each get a certain amount of space, but we can divide it up or share it however we want. The walls are movable like in hotel ballrooms. The "fixed" outer walls have computer screens built in. These can be made into "windows" by hooking them up to outside cameras.

ROBOTS—AND SKATEBOARDERS!—CAN USE THE RAMPS IN THE FOUNDERS DOME.

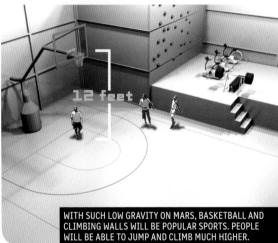

12 feet

WITH SUCH LOW GRAVITY ON MARS, BASKETBALL AND CLIMBING WALLS WILL BE POPULAR SPORTS. PEOPLE WILL BE ABLE TO JUMP AND CLIMB MUCH HIGHER.

MARS CAFÉ MENU

BREAKFAST

Sweet potato pancakes

Wheat or rice waffles with strawberry syrup

Hash brown potatoes

Scrambled tofu

Pita bread with peanut butter and strawberry jam

Cream of wheat or rice with rice milk

DINNER

Sweet potato and bean burrito with salsa

Sweet and sour tempeh [soy cakes]

Sloppy Joes
[texturized soy protein] on whole wheat
bun with carrot sticks

Stir-fry tofu, carrots, mushrooms, and cabbage

Tabouli salad
[chopped wheat, tomatoes, onions, parsley, mint]

Spaghetti with basil tomato or creamed kale
sauce and mushrooms

Soy tacos with tomato, lettuce, and onions

Creamy potato soup
with lettuce, spinach, and tomato salad

Hot and sour tofu soup with potato casserole

DESSERT

Peanut brittle

Sweet potato pie

Rice pudding

Tofu cheesecake

Strawberry tarts

Coconut ice cream

One camera gives us a view of the canyon walls to the south. Some of them rise nearly six miles (9.7 km) high! Tell the folks on Earth that Mars is simply the best place in the solar system for climbers.

Just below us is one of the cylindrical greenhouses that extend out from the main ring like fat flower petals. Only the south side is glass. The north side is bricked over to keep it warm inside.

Hey, quit bouncing on the bed! You don't want it to spring a leak! Water beds are comfortable. But if you really like to jump, you might fill your bed with air instead. But watch your head: You can jump really high in the low gravity!

Okay, that's enough for the tour. Let's go get some dinner. I hear the cook is making red Martian spaghetti tonight with coconut ice cream for dessert!

ACTIVITY: HOME ON MARS

So many new settlers are coming to Mars that it's time to build a new town. The city council has asked you to build them a sample of what the new town will look like. Do this activity to show off your design.

SUPPLIES

- A cereal box, or small shirt box
- Scissors
- Tape
- Unlined paper
- Red construction or crepe paper
- Empty 2-liter clear plastic soda or water bottle
- Plastic lid (coffee can) about 4 inches (10 cm) in diameter or a piece of cardboard cut this size
- Toilet paper tube
- Rocks, pebbles, or marbles
- Small toy people
- Small artificial plants or cutouts
- Downloaded printed image of Mars panorama or colored pencils to draw a background image

DIRECTIONS

1 Cut around the front of a cereal box and lift it back to use as a background lid. Secure the sides with tape. Alternatively, use the top of a shirt box and tape the lid to the outside so it sticks up.

2 Draw or download an image (or two depending on the size of your "lid") to use for the background. Tape it to the lid.

3 Cover the bottom of the box with red construction paper or crepe paper.

4 Cut the 2-liter plastic bottle 5 to 6 inches (12.5–15 cm) from the bottom. This will be your park or greenhouse "dome."

5 The plastic lid (or cardboard) will be the floor of your dome. Tape plants or toy figures or park benches/playground equipment on this and place under the dome.

6 Slit the toilet paper tube lengthwise. This is your tunnel from the dome to the rest of your town, which is underground. You might line it with colored paper or decorate it like a school hallway. It might have people or vehicles or animals inside.

7 Place robots (that might look like dinosaurs or other animals!), space vehicles, space-suited figures, and rocks outside the dome.

8 Give your town a name!

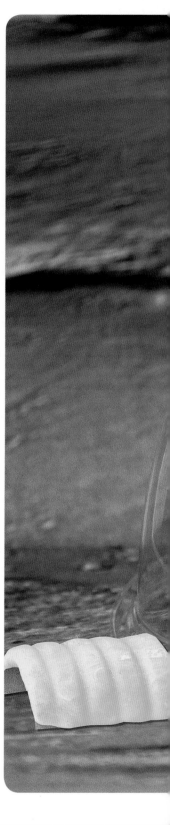

GREEN MARS

WE CAN LIVE ON MARS the way it is now. But it would be easier if we could work outside without space suits. To do that, we need thicker air.

Lots of sunshine zips past Mars every day. Giant mirrors in orbit could direct that sunshine to heat Mars's polar ice caps. A temperature increase of just a few degrees would thaw the carbon dioxide frozen there. Carbon dioxide is a "greenhouse" gas that traps heat. As the temperature rises, more carbon dioxide is released. That traps more heat. This is how Venus got so hot.

0   100   200   300   400   500

When we first arrive on Mars, the air will be too thin and the radiation level too high for people or plants to survive on the surface. People will live inside pressurized domes or cylinders covered by dirt or with filtered glass to block radiation.

During our first **100 years** on Mars, human factories will release gases. We may also crash comets into Mars to release ammonia and heat, and use space mirrors to melt the ice at the south pole. All these things will help thicken the air and warm Mars.

After about **200 years**, the air may be thick and warm enough to thaw the ice trapped in soil, and also block harmful radiation. Then microbes, algae, and lichens can grow on the surface. Clouds might get thick enough to produce snow or freezing rain.

If the mirrors aren't enough, we can knock an asteroid out of its orbit to slam into Mars. Some asteroids are rich in ammonia, another greenhouse gas. An impact would produce a lot more heat and carbon dioxide, too.

Once it is warm enough for water on the surface, plants can grow. Plants soak up carbon dioxide and make oxygen. After a thousand years, we may stand on the shore of a salty sea and breathe the fresh air.

600   700   800   900   1,000

Within about 600 years, the simple plants would have produced enough oxygen and prepared the soil enough that more complex plants like evergreens might take root. Enough ice will melt to create lakes and rivers.

Between 600 years and 1,000 years, Mars's atmosphere and surface will continue to change. More lakes and rivers will be filled with liquid water. More plants will begin to take root, creating more oxygen and using more carbon dioxide.

About 1,000 years after humans begin terraforming Mars, the air may be thick enough that they can go outdoors without a space suit. People may still require breathing masks depending on the levels of oxygen and other gases.

HERE I AM ON THE MOON WITH THE AMERICAN FLAG THAT NEIL ARMSTRONG AND I PLANTED DURING THE APOLLO 11 MISSION.

Will you be one of the first people to walk on Mars? The owner of the first Martian restaurant? Will your role be so important that they name a new Martian city after you?

It was an honor and a privilege for me to be part of the first human mission to the moon. As Neil Armstrong and I stood on the Sea of Tranquillity and looked up at our blue planet Earth, we saluted the hundreds of thousands of Americans who built our equipment, trained us, and made sure the bills got paid. The Apollo workers weren't all scientists and engineers. They were food testers and seamstresses and welders and accountants, too. Each member of the team played an important part in our success. We all shared in the 20th century's greatest achievement.

Making a home on the red planet will take the skills and talents of a new international team. Their achievement will be celebrated for thousands of years because they will have started the migration of humans to the stars. Will you place a plaque on Mars like the one we left on the moon that said "We came in peace for all mankind"? What would you say as you took that first step?

Neil and I did not see Apollo 11 as an ending. Rather, we saw our touchdown at Tranquillity Base as a first small step for humankind into the cosmos. I hope you do, too.

It is now time to continue that journey. July 20, 2019, marks the 50th anniversary of that first human landing on the moon. It's a perfect opportunity for the president of the United States to commit to establishing a permanent settlement on Mars within two decades. It's time to make a new home on Mars. Let's roll up our sleeves and begin!

—Buzz Aldrin

Books

Aldrin, Buzz, and Wendell Minor. *Look to the Stars.* New York: Putnam Juvenile, 2009.

Aldrin, Buzz, and Wendell Minor. *Reaching for the Moon.* New York: HarperCollins, 2008.

Bennett, Jeffrey, and Alan Okamoto. *Max Goes to Mars: A Science Adventure with Max the Dog.* Boulder: Big Kid Science, 2003.

Dyson, Marianne. *Home on the Moon: Living on a Space Frontier.* Washington, D.C.: National Geographic Society, 2003.

Dyson, Marianne. *Space and Astronomy: Decade by Decade.* New York: Facts on File, 2007.

Hartmann, William K. *A Traveler's Guide to Mars: The Mysterious Landscapes of the Red Planet.* New York: Workman Publishing, 2003.

Kaufman, Marc. *Mars Up Close: Inside the Curiosity Mission.* Washington, D.C.: National Geographic Society, 2014.

O'Brien, Patrick. *You Are the First Kid on Mars.* New York: Putnam Juvenile, 2009.

Rusch, Elizabeth. *The Mighty Mars Rovers: The Incredible Adventures of Spirit and Opportunity* (Scientists in the Field Series). Boston: Houghton Mifflin Harcourt (HMH) Books for Young Readers, 2012.

Turner, Pamela S. *Life on Earth—and Beyond: An Astrobiologist's Quest.* Watertown, MA: Charlesbridge, 2008.

Websites

Aldrin, Buzz. Official website. buzzaldrin.com. Links to videos of events. Schedule of appearances.

Dyson, Marianne. Official website. mdyson.com. Information about author visits, books, stories, reviews, and activities.

ESA. "Robotic Exploration of Mars." exploration.esa.int/mars. Latest news and images from European spacecraft studying Mars.

Indian Space Research Organisation. "Mars Orbiter Mission." isro.gov.in/pslv-c25-mars-orbiter-mission. Latest information about India's first Mars mission.

NASA. "Mars Exploration." mars.nasa.gov. Latest news and images from American spacecraft studying Mars.

NASA. "Solar System Exploration: Mars Overview." solarsystem.nasa.gov/planets/profile.cfm?Object=Mars. Homework help for future Martians!

National Earth Science Teachers Association. "Windows to the Universe: The Orbit of Mars." Mars and Earth positions for any date past or future. windows2universe.org/mars/mars_orbit.html.

National Geographic Kids. "Mission to Mars." kids.national geographic.com/explore/space/mission-to-mars.

For adults, now in paperback!

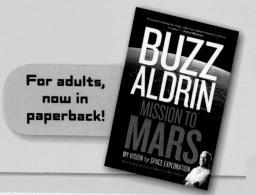

AIR PRESSURE: the force of air pressing on a surface

APOLLO: a series of American space missions between 1968 and 1972. Apollo 11 was the first mission to land humans, including Buzz Aldrin, on the moon.

AREOLOGY: the study of Mars

ARES: the Greeks' name for Mars, the god of war

CYCLER: a spacecraft that follows a repeating path between two worlds such as Earth and Mars

ECLIPTIC: the sun's apparent path among the stars over the course of a year

ESA: European Space Agency, an organization of 20 member states

FROST: ice crystals that form on the ground when it is below freezing

GEMINI: a series of American space missions between 1965 and 1966 that focused on rendezvous in preparation for the Apollo missions to the moon

GEOTHERMAL: power using the heat of the earth below ground to generate electrical power

HABITAT [HAB]: a place created for people and animals to live, and which provides the resources needed for survival

NASA: National Aeronautics and Space Administration, a government organization in charge of space activities for the United States

NUTRIENTS: elements needed for life and growth

ORGANIC MOLECULES: molecules that contain carbon, which is necessary for life as we know it

RADIATION: high-energy light waves or atomic particles (cosmic rays) produced by stars

RENDEZVOUS: the meeting of two people or things

RESOURCES: naturally occurring materials

RETRO-ROCKET: a small rocket used to slow down a spacecraft

SPECTRUM: a pattern of colors produced when light shines through a prism

TERRAFORM: creating an environment that is good for Earth plants and animals

TRANSPORT: a spacecraft that takes people from one location in space to another

WINDOW: the best time to launch a rocket, usually when it requires the least energy

Quotation Credits

title page: National Geographic Society. "First Person: What I'm Learning on a Simulated Mars Mission." voices.nationalgeographic.com/2014/03/25/first-person-what-im-learning-on-a-simulated-mars-mission. March 25, 2014.

page 11: National Geographic Society. "Explorers Bio: Brendan Mullan." nationalgeographic.com/explorers/bios/brendan-mullan.

page 15: Kaufman, Marc. *Mars Up Close: Inside the Curiosity Mission.* Washington, D.C.: National Geographic Society, 2014. p. 9.

page 26: Rosenberg, Jennifer. "War of the Worlds Radio Broadcast Causes Panic" (Part 2). About Education. history1900s.about.com/od/1930s/a/warofworlds.htm. Downloaded September 11, 2014.

page 29: Lowell, Percival. *The Solar System: Six Lectures Delivered at the Massachusetts Institute of Technology in December, 1902.* Boston/New York: Houghton, Mifflin and Company, 1903.

page 37: Davidson, Keay. *Carl Sagan: A Life.* New York: John Wiley and Sons, 1999. pp. 276-77.

page 39: Dyson, Marianne. *Space and Astronomy: Decade by Decade.* New York: Facts on File, 2007. p. 222.

page 41: National Geographic Society. "Explorers Bio: Bethany Ehlmann." nationalgeographic.com/explorers/bios/bethany-ehlmann.

page 44: The White House. "President Bush Announces New Vision for Space Exploration Program." history.nasa.gov/Bush%20SEP.htm. January 14, 2004.

page 46: Aldrin, Buzz, and Leonard David. *Mission to Mars: My Vision for Space Exploration.* Washington, D.C.: National Geographic Society, 2013. p. 245.

page 47: Kennedy Space Center. "President Outlines Exploration Goals, Promise." nasa.gov/about/obama speechfeature.html. April 15, 2010.

page 63: National Geographic Society. "Explorers Bio: Constance Adams." nationalgeographic.com/explorers/bios/constance-adams.

Photo and Image Credits

Front cover and spine: Peter Bollinger; Back cover: NASA/JSC; Front flap: Peter Bollinger; Back flap: (Buzz Aldrin) Katy Winn/Corbis; (Marianne Dyson) Marianne Dyson; (robot) Peter Bollinger; 1, ESA, C. Carreau; 1, NASA/JPL-Caltech/MSSS ; 2–3, NASA/JPL/Arizona State University, R. Luk; 4–5, NASA/JPL-Caltech/MSSS; 6–7, NASA/JPL-Caltech; 7 (UPRT), NASA; 10–11 (UP), David Aguilar; 11 (LOLE), MPI/Stringer; 11 (LORT), NASA; 12 (LO), Vereshchagin Dmitry/Shutterstock; 12 (UPLE), NASA; 12 (bug spray), homeworks255/iStockphoto; 12 (jacket), Karkas/Shutterstock; 12 (lawn mower), Cimmerian/iStockphoto; 12 (umbrella), 2happy/iStockphoto; 13, NASA/Bill Ingalls; 14 (LORT), SPACEX; 14 (LOLE), Ken Kremer; 15, NASA; 17 (UP), Artwork done for NASA by Pat Rawlings, of SAIC; 17 (LO), NASA/JPL-Caltech/University of Arizona; 18–19, Mark Thiessen, NGS; 20 (LOLE), NASA; 20–21 (UP), Imageman/Shutterstock; 21 (LORT), Buzz Aldrin/Twitter; 21, Loskutnikov/Shutterstock; 21 (UPRT), NASA image and animation by Robert Simmon and Jesse Allen, based on data from Marshall Space Flight Center Solar Physics Group and the SOHO Michelson Doppler Imager Project; 21 (UPLE), NASA; 23 (UP), Used by permission from the Buzz Aldrin Photo Archive; 23 (LO), Mark Thiessen, NGS; 26–27 (UP), MasPix/Alamy; 26 (LORT), World History Archive/Alamy; 27 (LOCTR), World History Archive/Alamy; 27 (LORT), World History Archive/Alamy; 28–29 (UP), Aeronautical Chart and Information Center (U.S.); 29 (UPRT), Everett Collection Inc./Alamy; 31 (LO), Mark Thiessen, NGS; 32, Science Source; 33 (LORT), Bettmann/Corbis; 33 (LOCTR), NASA; 36–37, JP Laffont/Sygma/Corbis; 37 (RT), NASA; 38, NASA/JPL/CNP/Corbis; 38 (LORT), NASA; 38 (LO), NASA; 39 (LORT), NASA/JSC/Stanford University ; 40–41, NASA/Jet Propulsion Laboratory; 42 (LO), AFP/Getty Images; 43 (LO), Corby Waste; 44 (LORT), NASA/JPL/Cornell University; 44 (LOLE), Photri Images/Alamy; 45, NASA; 46, Pete Souza/The White House; 46 (LORT), NASA; 47, NASA; 48 (LORT), NG Images/Alamy; 48 (UP CTR), NASA; 48 (LORT), NASA; 48 (UPLE), NASA; 48 (LORT), Julian Baum/Science Source; 48–49 (UP CTR), Detlev van Ravenswaay/Science Source; 49 (UPLE), NASA; 49 (LOLE), AFP/Getty Images; 49 (LOCTR), Science Source; 49 (LORT), NASA; 49 (UP CTR), Detlev van Ravenswaay/Science Source; 49 (LOLE), Science Source; 50–51, NG Maps; 55 (UP), MOLA Science Team; 55 (LORT), MOLA Science Team; 56–57 (LE CTR), NASA/JPL/Arizona State University; 57 (LE CTR), William Litant/MIT ; 58 (LO), Jim Olive/Polaris/Newscom; 59, Pat Rawlings; 60, Mark Thiessen/National Geographic Creative; 60 (UP CTR RT), Becky Hale, NGS; 61, Mark Thiessen/NGS; 62–63 (LO), NASA/JPL-Caltech/Cornell; 63 (UPRT), NASA/JPL-Caltech/MSSS; 65 (LO), NASA/JPL/Caltech, Artist Corby Waste, 1999; 65 (UP), parameter/iStockphoto; 66–67, Mark Thiessen/NGS; 68, Tom Peters; 69, UniversalImagesGroup/Contributor/Getty Images; 70–71 (UPRT), ESA/DLR/Freie Universitat Berlin; 70 (LOLE), NASA/JPL-Caltech/MSSS 2004 rover image courtesy of NASA/JPL-Caltech/Cornell; 71 (LORT), NASA/JPL/Los Alamos National Laboratory; 72 (LE), NASA/JPL-Caltech/University of Arizona; 72 (RT), NASA/JPL-Caltech/University of Arizona; 73, Mark Thiessen/NGS; 74, Pat Rawlings; 75, Mark Thiessen/NGS; 76, Diane Cook & Len Jenshel/Corbis; 77, NASA/Goddard Space Flight Center Scientific Visualization Studio; 78, NASA; 79, De Agostini Picture Library/Contributor/Getty Images; 79 (LO), NASA/JPL-Caltech/MSSS/ASU; 83 (LOLE), NASA; 83 (LOLE), Feverpitched/Dreamstime.com; 83 (UPRT), NASA; 85, Pavel Gramatikov/Dreamstime.com; 88–89, Stefan Morrell/National Geographic Creative; 90, NASA; 91 (cover background) NASA/JPL-Caltech; 91 (stars) thrash-em/Shutterstock; 91 (Buzz Aldrin) Rebecca Hale; 96, NASA

This book is dedicated to the **Generation Mars kids** in my life—my great-grandsons NATHANIEL and BENJAMIN SCHUSS and my two mascots—BRIELLE and LOGAN KORP.

—BUZZ ALDRIN

I would like to thank the editorial team at National Geographic, NANCY FERESTEN, JENNIFER EMMETT, and SHELBY ALINSKY, for continuing to share **my love of space exploration** with CHILDREN around the world. Thanks also to my friends at the LUNAR AND PLANETARY INSTITUTE, NASA, and in SCBWI for their encouragement and support while researching this book.

—MARIANNE J. DYSON

Staff for This Book
Shelby Alinsky, *Project Editor*
Julide Obuz Dengel, *Art Director*
Bri Bertoia, *Photo Editor*
Bea Jackson, *Designer*
Paige Towler, *Editorial Assistant*
Sanjida Rashid and Rachel Kenny, *Design Production Assistants*
Colm McKeveny, *Rights Clearance Specialists*
Grace Hill, *Managing Editor*
Joan Gossett, *Senior Production Editor*
Lewis R. Bassford, *Production Manager*
Bobby Barr, *Manager, Production Services*
Susan Borke, *Legal and Business Affairs*

Published by the National Geographic Society
Gary E. Knell, *President and CEO*
John M. Fahey, *Chairman of the Board*
Melina Gerosa Bellows, *Chief Education Officer*

Declan Moore, *Chief Media Officer*
Hector Sierra, *Senior Vice President and General Manager, Book Division*

Senior Management Team, Kids Publishing and Media
Nancy Laties Feresten, *Senior Vice President*; Jennifer Emmett, *Vice President, Editorial Director, Kids Books*; Julie Vosburgh Agnone, *Vice President, Editorial Operations*; Rachel Buchholz, *Editor and Vice President, NG Kids magazine*; Michelle Sullivan, *Vice President, Kids Digital*; Eva Absher-Schantz, *Design Director*; Jay Sumner, *Photo Director*; Hannah August, *Marketing Director*; R. Gary Colbert, *Production Director*

Digital
Anne McCormack, *Director*; Laura Goertzel, Sara Zeglin, *Producers*; Jed Winer, *Special Projects Assistant*; Emma Rigney, *Creative Producer*; Bianca Bowman, *Assistant Producer*; Natalie Jones, *Senior Product Manager*

The National Geographic Society is one of the world's largest nonprofit scientific and educational organizations. Founded in 1888 to "increase and diffuse geographic knowledge," the Society's mission is to inspire people to care about the planet. It reaches more than 400 million people worldwide each month through its official journal, *National Geographic*, and other magazines; National Geographic Channel; television documentaries; music; radio; films; books; DVDs; maps; exhibitions; live events; school publishing programs; interactive media; and merchandise. National Geographic has funded more than 10,000 scientific research, conservation, and exploration projects and supports an education program promoting geographic literacy.

For more information, please visit nationalgeographic.com, call 1-800-NGS LINE (647-5463), or write to the following address:
National Geographic Society
1145 17th Street N.W.
Washington, D.C. 20036-4688 U.S.A.

Visit us online at nationalgeographic.com/books

For librarians and teachers: ngchildrensbooks.org

More for kids from National Geographic:
kids.nationalgeographic.com

For information about special discounts for bulk purchases, please contact National Geographic Books Special Sales: ngspecsales@ngs.org

For rights or permissions inquiries, please contact National Geographic Books Subsidiary Rights: ngbookrights@ngs.org

Trade edition ISBN: 978-1-4263-2206-8
Reinforced library edition ISBN: 978-1-4263-2207-5

Printed in Hong Kong
15/THK/1